The Castle Lectures in E̶t̶h̶i̶c̶s̶,̶

Ethics, Politics and Economics

How Democratic
Is the
American
Constitution?

SECOND EDITION

———————————

Robert A. Dahl

Yale University Press / New Haven & London

Published with assistance from the foundation established in memory of
Philip Hamilton McMillan of the Class of 1894, Yale College.

This Nota Bene edition published 2003 by Yale University Press.
First Edition published 2002 by Yale University Press.
Second Edition copyright © 2003 by Yale University.
First Edition copyright © 2002 by Yale University.

Designed by James J. Johnson and set in New Caledonia and
Bulmer types by Integrated Publishing Solutions.
Printed in the United States of America.

For information about this and other Yale University Press publications,
please contact:
    U.S. office   sales.press@yale.edu
    Europe office   sales@yaleup.co.uk

Library of Congress Control Number: 2003106483
ISBN 978-0-300-09524-1 (pbk)

A catalogue record for this book is available from the British Library.

10 9 8 7 6

Parts of this book were given as a series of Castle Lectures in Yale's Program in Ethics, Politics, and Economics, delivered by Robert Dahl at Yale University in 2000.

The Castle Lectures, endowed by Mr. John K. Castle, honor his ancestor, the Reverend James Pierpont, one of Yale's founders. Given by prominent public figures, the lectures are intended to promote reflection on the moral foundations of society and government and to enhance understanding of ethical issues facing individuals in our complex modern society.

Contents

Acknowledgments

THE INVITATION TO DELIVER THE CASTLE LECTURES AT Yale provided me with an incentive for bringing into focus views about the American Constitution that I had gradually formed over many years. Though I had set forth some of my arguments in various essays and book chapters, others remained largely implicit or undeveloped until I drafted the lectures. This book embodies the substance of the Castle Lectures, slightly revised and enlarged, that I delivered in the early fall of 2000.

For extending to me the invitation to deliver the lectures, I am indebted to Geoffrey Garrett, director of the Program in Ethics, Politics, and Economics. To both him and Ian Shapiro I want to express my appreciation for their warm endorsement of the subject I proposed for my lectures.

For her invaluable research assistance I am indebted to Jennifer Smith.

For their helpful queries, corrections, or contributions I also want to thank Wendell Bell, Kai Erikson, Fred Greenstein, Steven Hill, Malcolm Jewell, Joseph LaPalombara, Rogers Smith, and, at Yale University Press, Ali Peterson for her sensitive editing and Larisa Heimert for her skillful and energetic help in conducting the manuscript through the publishing process.

Finally, let me take this opportunity to express my thanks to those members of the audience whose questions and comments enabled me to discover aspects of my presentation that would benefit, in this published version, from greater clarification or more extensive treatment.

CHAPTER 1

Introduction:
Fundamental Questions

Y AIM IN THIS BRIEF BOOK IS NOT TO PROPOSE changes in the American Constitution but to suggest changes in the way we *think* about our constitution. In that spirit, I'll begin by posing a simple question: *Why should we Americans uphold our Constitution?*

Well, an American citizen might reply, it has been our constitution ever since it was written in 1787 by a group of exceptionally wise men and was then ratified by conventions in all the states.[1] But this answer only leads to a further question.

To understand what lies behind that next question, I want to recall how the Constitutional Convention that met in Philadelphia during the summer of 1787 was made up. Although we tend to assume that all thirteen states sent delegates, in fact Rhode Island refused to attend, and the delegates from New Hampshire didn't arrive until some weeks after the Convention opened. As a result, several crucial votes in June and July were taken with only eleven state delegations in attendance. Moreover, the votes were counted by states, and although most of the time most state delegations agreed on a single position, on occasion they were too divided internally to cast a vote.

My question, then, is this: Why should we feel bound today by a document produced more than two centuries ago by a group of fifty-five mortal men, actually signed by only thirty-nine, a fair number of whom were slaveholders, and adopted in only thirteen states by the votes of fewer than two thousand men, all of whom are long since dead and mainly forgotten?[2]

Our citizen might respond that we Americans are free, after all, to alter our constitution by amendment and have often done so. Therefore our present constitution is ultimately based on the consent of those of us living today.

But before we accept this reply, let me pose another question: Have we Americans ever had an opportunity to express our considered will on our constitutional system? For example, how many readers of these lines have ever participated in a referendum that asked them whether they wished to continue to be governed under the existing constitution? The answer, of course, is: none.

Our citizen might now fall back on another line of argument: Why should we change a constitution that has served and continues to serve us well?

Although this is surely a reasonable line of argument, it does suggest still another question: By what *standards* does our constitution serve us well? In particular, how well does our constitutional system meet *democratic* standards of the present day? I'll turn to this question in the next chapter.

And if our constitution is as good as most Americans seem to think it is, why haven't other democratic countries copied it? As we'll see in Chapter 3, every other advanced democratic country has adopted a constitutional system very different from ours. Why?

If our constitutional system turns out to be unique among the constitutions of other advanced democratic countries, is it any better for its differences, or is it worse? Or don't the differences matter? I'll explore this difficult question in the fourth chapter.

Suppose we find little or no evidence to support the view that our constitutional system is superior to the systems of other comparable democratic countries, and that in some respects it may actually perform rather worse. What should we conclude?

As one part of an answer, I am going to suggest that we begin to view our American Constitution as nothing more or less than a set of basic institutions and practices designed to the best of our abilities for the purpose of attaining democratic values. But if an important democratic value is *political equality,* won't political equality threaten the rights and liberties we prize? In Chapter 5, I'll argue that this view—famously defended by Tocqueville, among others—is based on a misunderstanding of the relationship between democracy and fundamental rights.

Yet the question remains: if our constitution is in some important ways defective by democratic standards, should we change it, and how? As I said, my aim here is not so much to suggest changes in the existing constitution as to encourage us to change the way we *think* about it, whether it be the existing one, an amended version of it, or a new and more democratic constitution. That said, in my final chapter I'll comment briefly on some possible changes and on the obstacles to achieving them.

★ ★ ★

BEFORE TURNING TO THESE QUESTIONS, I NEED TO DISpose of two matters. One is purely terminological. In discussing the formation of the constitution at the Convention in 1787, I shall refer to the delegates as the Framers, not, as is more common, the Founding Fathers. I do so because many of the men who reasonably might be listed among the Founding Fathers—including such notables as John Adams, Samuel Adams, Tom Paine, and Thomas Jefferson—were not at the Convention. (By my count, only eight of the fifty-five delegates to the Convention had also signed the Declaration of Independence.)

The second matter is both terminological and substantive. Some readers may argue that the Founding Fathers (including the Framers) intended to create a republic, not a democracy. From this premise, according to a not uncommon belief among Americans, it follows that the United States is not a democracy but a republic. Although this belief is sometimes supported on the authority of a principal architect of the Constitution, James Madison, it is, for reasons I explain in Appendix A, mistaken.

But even more important, the conclusion does not follow from the premise. Whatever the intentions of the Framers may have been, we would hardly feel bound by them today if we believed that they were morally, politically, and constitutionally wrong. Indeed, more than two centuries of experience demonstrates that whenever a sufficiently large and influential number of Americans conclude that the views of the Framers *were* wrong, they will change the constitution. Even if the Framers did not intend their constitution to abolish slavery, when later generations concluded that slavery could no longer be tolerated and must be abolished, they changed the constitution to conform with their beliefs.

Even if some of the Framers leaned more toward the idea of an aristocratic republic than a democratic republic, they soon discovered that under the leadership of James Madison, among others, Americans would rapidly undertake to create a more democratic republic, and in doing so they would begin almost immediately to change the constitutional system the Framers had created.

CHAPTER 2

What the Framers Couldn't Know

———————◆———————

WISE AS THE FRAMERS WERE, THEY WERE
necessarily limited by their profound ignorance.

I say this with no disrespect, for like many others I
believe that among the Framers were many men of exceptional talent and public virtue. Indeed, I regard
James Madison as our greatest political scientist and
his generation of political leaders as perhaps our most
richly endowed with wisdom, public virtue, and devo-
tion to lives of public service. In the months and weeks
before the Constitutional Convention assembled "on
Monday the 14th of May, A.D. 1787. [*sic*] and in the
eleventh year of the independence of the United States
of America, at the State-House in the city of Philadel-

phia,"[1] Madison studied the best sources as carefully as a top student preparing for a major exam.[2] But even James Madison could not foresee the future of the American republic, nor could he draw on knowledge that might be gained from later experiences with democracy in America and elsewhere.

It is no detraction from the genius of Leonardo da Vinci to say that given the knowledge available in his time he could not possibly have designed a workable airplane—much less the spacecraft that now bears his name. Nor, given the knowledge available in 1903, could the Wright brothers have built the Boeing 707. Although like many others I greatly admire Benjamin Franklin, I recognize that his knowledge of electricity was infinitesimal compared with that of a first-year student in electrical engineering—or, for that matter, the electrician who takes care of my occasional wiring problems. In fact, on that famous first experiment with the kite, Franklin was lucky to have escaped alive. None of us, I expect, would hire an electrician equipped only with Franklin's knowledge to do our wiring, nor would we propose to make a trip from New York to London in the Wright brothers' aircraft. Leonardo, Franklin, the Wright brothers were great innovators in their time, but they could not draw on knowledge that was still to be accumulated in the years and centuries to come.

The knowledge of the Framers—some of them, certainly—may well have been the best available in

1787. But reliable knowledge about constitutions appropriate to a large representative republic was, at best, meager. History had produced no truly relevant models of representative government on the scale the United States had already attained, not to mention the scale it would reach in the years to come. As much as many of the delegates admired the British constitution, it was far from a suitable model. Nor could the Roman Republic provide much of a guide. The famous Venetian Republic, illustrious though it had been, was governed by a hereditary aristocracy of fewer than two thousand men and was already tottering: a decade after the Convention an upstart Corsican would knock it over in a featherweight military attack. Whatever knowledge the delegates could gain from historical experience was, then, only marginally relevant at best.

Leaping into the Unknown

Among the important aspects of an unforeseeable future, four broad historical developments would yield some potential knowledge that the Framers necessarily lacked and that, had they possessed it, might well have led them to a different constitutional design.

First, a peaceful democratic revolution was soon to alter fundamentally the conditions under which their constitutional system would function.

Second, partly in response to that continuing revolution, new democratic political institutions would fundamentally alter and reconstruct the framework they had so carefully designed.

Third, when democratization unfolded in Europe and in other English-speaking countries during the two centuries to come, constitutional arrangements would arise that were radically different from the American system. Within a generation or two, even the British constitution would bear little resemblance to the one the Framers knew—or thought they knew—and in many respects admired and hoped to imitate.

Fourth, ideas and beliefs about what democracy requires, and thus what a democratic republic requires, would continue to evolve down to the present day and probably beyond. Both in the way we understand the meaning of "democracy" and in the practices and institutions we regard as necessary to it, democracy is not a static system. Democratic ideas and institutions as they unfolded in the two centuries after the American Constitutional Convention would go far beyond the conceptions of the Framers and would even transcend the views of such early democrats as Jefferson and Madison, who helped to initiate moves toward a more democratic republic.

I shall consider each of these developments in later chapters. But first I want to indicate some of the practical limitations on what the Framers could reasonably achieve.

What the Framers Couldn't Do

The Framers were not only limited by, so to speak, their inevitable ignorance. They were also crucially limited by the opportunities available to them.

We can be profoundly grateful for one crucial restriction: the Framers were limited to considering only a *republican* form of government. They were constrained not only by their own belief in the superiority of a republican government over all others but also by their conviction that the high value they placed on republicanism was overwhelmingly shared by American citizens in all the states. Whatever else the Framers might be free to do, they well knew that they could not possibly propose a monarchy or a government ruled by an aristocracy. As the Massachusetts delegate Elbridge Gerry put it, "There was not a one-thousand part of our fellow citizens who were not against every approach toward monarchy."[3] The only delegate who was recorded by Madison[4] as looking with favor on monarchy was Alexander Hamilton, whose injudicious expression of support for that heartily unpopular institution may have greatly reduced his influence at the Convention, as it was to haunt him later.[5] Hardly more acceptable was an adaptation of aristocratic ideas to an American constitution. During the deliberations about the Senate, Gouverneur Morris of Pennsylvania explored the possibility of drawing its members from an American equivalent of the British aristocracy.[6] But it soon became obvious that the delegates could not agree on just who these American aristocrats might be, and in any case they well knew that the overwhelming bulk of American citizens would simply not tolerate such a government.

A second immovable limit was the existence of the thirteen states, with still more states to come. A constitutional solution that would be available in most of the countries that were to develop into mature and stable democracies—a unitary system with exclusive sovereignty lodged in the central government, as in Britain and Sweden, for example—was simply out of the question. The need for a federal rather than a unitary republic was therefore not justified by a principle adduced from general historical experience, much less from political theory. It was just a self-evident fact. If Americans were to be united in a single country, it was obvious to all that a federal or confederal system was inescapable. Whether the states would remain as fundamental constituents was therefore never a serious issue at the Convention; the only contested question was just how much autonomy, if any, they would yield to the central government.[7]

The delegates had to confront still another stubborn limit: the need to engage in fundamental compromises in order to secure agreement on any constitution at all. The necessity for compromise and the opportunities this gave for coalitions and logrolling meant that the Constitution could not possibly reflect a coherent, unified theory of government. Compromises were necessary because, like the country at large, members of the convention held different views on some very basic issues.

Slavery.   One, of course, was the future of slavery. Most of the delegates from the five southern states were adamantly opposed to any constitutional provision that might endanger the institution. Although the delegates from the other seven states were hardly of one mind about slavery, it was perfectly obvious to them that the only condition on which coexistence would be acceptable to the delegates from the southern states would be the preservation of slavery. Consequently, if these delegates wanted a federal constitution they would have to yield, no matter what their beliefs about slavery. And so they did. Although some delegates who signed the final document abhorred slavery, they nevertheless accepted its continuation as the price of a stronger federal government.

Representation in the Senate.   Another conflict of views that could not be settled without a one-sided compromise resulted from the adamant refusal of the delegates from the small states to accept any constitution that did not provide for equal representation in the Senate. The opponents of equal representation included two of the most illustrious members of the Convention, James Madison and James Wilson, who were also among the chief architects of the Constitution. Both men bitterly opposed what seemed to them an arbitrary, unnecessary, and unjustifiable limit on national majorities. As Alexander Hamilton remarked about this conflict: "As states are a collection of individual men which ought we to respect most, the rights of the people composing them, or the artificial beings resulting from the composition. Nothing could be more preposterous or absurd than to sacrifice the former to the latter. It has been sd. that if the smaller States renounce their *equality*, they renounce at the same time their *liberty*. The truth is it is a contest for power, not for liberty. Will the men composing the small States be less free than those composing the larger."[8]

Let me give you a flavor of the elevated discussion that preceded the victory of the small states. Here is Gunning Bedford of Delaware on June 30:

> The large states dare not dissolve the Confederation. If they do the small ones will find some foreign ally of more honor and good faith, who will take them by the hand and do them justice.

To which Rufus King of Massachusetts replied:

> I cannot sit down, without taking some notice of the language of the honorable gentleman from Delaware. . . . It was not I who with a vehemence unprecedented in this House, declared himself ready to turn his hopes from our common Country, and court the protection of some foreign hand. . . . I am grieved that such a thought has entered into his heart. . . . For myself whatever might be my distress, I would never court relief from a foreign power.[9]

Faced with the refusal of the small states to accept anything less, Madison, Wilson, Hamilton, and the other opponents of equal representation finally accepted compromise of principle as the price of a constitution. The solution of equal representation was not, then, a product of constitutional theory, high principle, or grand design. It was nothing more than a practical outcome of a hard bargain that its opponents finally agreed to in order to achieve a constitution.[10]

Incidentally, this conflict illustrates some of the complexities of voting coalitions at the Constitutional Convention, for the faction opposed to equal representation in the Senate included four strange bedfellows: Madison, Wilson, Hamilton, and Gouverneur Morris. Although all four generally supported moves to strengthen the federal government, Madison and Wilson usually endorsed proposals that leaned toward a more democratic republic, while Hamilton and Morris tended to support a more aristocratic republic.

Undemocratic Elements in the Framers' Constitution

It was within these limits, then, that the Framers constructed the Constitution. Not surprisingly, it fell far short of the requirements that later generations would find necessary and desirable in a democratic republic. Judged from later, more democratic perspectives, the Constitution of the Framers contained at least seven important shortcomings.

Slavery.   First, it neither forbade slavery nor empowered Congress to do so. In fact, the compromise on slavery not only denied Congress the effective power to prohibit the importation of slaves before 1808[11] but it gave constitutional sanction to one of the most morally objectionable byproducts of a morally repulsive institution: the Fugitive Slave laws, according to which a slave who managed to escape to a free state had to be returned to the slaveholder, whose property the slave remained.[12] That it took three-quarters of a century and a sanguinary civil war before slavery was abolished should at the least make us doubt whether the document of the Framers ought to be regarded as holy writ.

Suffrage. Second, the constitution failed to guarantee the right of suffrage, leaving the qualifications of suffrage to the states.[13] It implicitly left in place the exclusion of half the population—women—as well as African Americans and Native Americans.[14] As we know, it took a century and a half before women were constitutionally guaranteed the right to vote, and nearly two centuries before a president and Congress could overcome the effective veto of a minority of states in order to pass legislation intended to guarantee the voting rights of African Americans.

Election of the president. Third, the executive power was vested in a president whose selection, according to the intentions and design of the Framers, was to be insulated from both popular majorities and congressional control. As we'll see, the Framers' main design for achieving that purpose—a body of presidential electors composed of men of exceptional wisdom and virtue who would choose the chief executive unswayed by popular opinion—was almost immediately cast into the dustbin of history by leaders sympathetic with the growing democratic impulses of the American people, among them James Madison himself. Probably nothing the Framers did illustrates more sharply their inability to foresee the shape that politics would assume in a democratic republic. (I shall say more about the electoral college in a later chapter.)

Choosing senators.   Fourth, senators were to be chosen not by the people but by the state legislatures, for a term of six years.[15] Although this arrangement fell short of the ambitions of delegates like Gouverneur Morris who wanted to construct an aristocratic upper house, it would help to ensure that senators would be less responsive to popular majorities and perhaps more sensitive to the needs of property holders. Members of the Senate would thus serve as a check on the Representatives, who were all subject to popular elections every two years.[16]

Equal representation in the Senate.   The attempt to create a Senate that would be a republican version of the aristocratic House of Lords was derailed, as we have seen, by a prolonged and bitter dispute over an entirely different question: Should the states be equally represented in Congress or should members of both houses be allocated according to population? This question not only gave rise to one of the most disruptive issues of the Convention, but it resulted in a fifth undemocratic feature of the constitution. As a consequence

of the famous—or from a democratic point of view, in-
famous—"Connecticut Compromise" each state was,
as we have seen, awarded the same number of senators, without respect to population. Although this
arrangement failed to protect the fundamental rights
and interests of the most deprived minorities, some
strategically placed and highly privileged minorities—
slaveholders, for example—gained disproportionate
power over government polices at the expense of less
privileged minorities. (I shall come back to this element in the constitution in a later chapter.)

Judicial power. Sixth, the constitution of the
Framers failed to limit the powers of the judiciary to
declare as unconstitutional laws that had been properly passed by Congress and signed by the president.
What the delegates intended in the way of judicial review will remain forever unclear; probably many delegates were unclear in their own minds, and to the extent that they discussed the question at all, they were
not in full agreement. But probably a majority accepted the view that the federal courts should rule on
the constitutionality of state and federal laws in cases
brought before them. Nevertheless, it is likely that
a substantial majority intended that federal judges
should not participate in making government laws and
policies, a responsibility that clearly belonged not to
the judiciary but to the legislative branch. Their opposition to any policy-making role for the judiciary is
strongly indicated by their response to a proposal in
the Virginia Plan that "the Executive and a convenient

number of the National Judiciary, ought to compose a council of revision" empowered to veto acts of the National Legislature. Though this provision was vigorously defended by Madison and Mason, it was voted down, 6 states to 3.[17]

A judicial veto is one thing; judicial legislation is quite another. Whatever some of the delegates may have thought about the advisability of justices sharing with the executive the authority to veto laws passed by Congress, I am fairly certain that none would have given the slightest support to a proposal that judges should themselves have the power to legislate, to make national policy. However, the upshot of their work was that in the guise of reviewing the constitutionality of state and congressional actions or inactions, the federal judiciary would later engage in what in some instances could only be called judicial policy-making—or, if you like, judicial legislation.[18]

Congressional power.   Finally, the powers of Congress were limited in ways that could, and at times did, prevent the federal government from regulating or controlling the economy by means that all modern democratic governments have adopted. Without the power to tax incomes, for example, fiscal policy, not to say measures like Social Security, would be impossible. And regulatory actions—over railroad rates, air safety, food and drugs, banking, minimum wages, and many other policies—had no clear constitutional authorization. Although it would be anachronistic to charge the Framers with lack of foresight in these matters,[19] unless the constitution could be altered by amendment or by heroic reinterpretation of its provisions—presumably by what I have just called judicial legislation—it would prevent representatives of later majorities from adopting the policies they believed were necessary to achieve efficiency, fairness, and security in a complex post-agrarian society.

Enlightened as the Framers' constitution may have been by the standards of the eighteenth century, future generations with more democratic aspirations would find some of its undemocratic features objectionable—and even unacceptable. The public expression of these growing democratic aspirations was not long in coming.

Even Madison did not, and probably could not, predict the peaceful democratic revolution that was about to begin. For the American revolution was soon to enter into a new and unforeseen phase.

The Framers' Constitution Meets
Emergent Democratic Beliefs

We may tend to think of the American republic and its constitution as solely the product of leaders inspired by extraordinary wisdom and virtue. Yet without a citizenry committed to republican principles of government and capable of governing themselves in accordance with those principles, the constitution would soon have been little more than a piece of paper. As historical experience would reveal, in countries where democratic beliefs were fragile or absent, constitutions did indeed become little more than pieces of paper— soon violated, soon forgotten.

The American democratic republic was not created nor could it have been long maintained by leaders alone, gifted as they may have been. It was they, to be sure, who designed a framework suitable, as they thought, for a republic. But it was the American people, and the leaders responsive to them, who ensured that the new republic would rapidly become a *democratic* republic.

The proto-republican phase. The ideas, practices, and political culture necessary to sustain a republican government were by no means unfamiliar to Americans. Unlike some countries that have moved almost overnight from dictatorship to democratic forms, and often soon thereafter to chaos and back to dictatorship, by 1787 the Americans had already accumulated a century and a half of experience in the arts of government.

The long colonial period had provided opportunities to both leaders and many men of ordinary rank to become acquainted with the requirements of self-government, both in the direct form of a town meeting and through electing representatives to the colonial legislatures.[20] We easily forget that although in its two famous opening paragraphs the Declaration of Independence laid down some new and audacious claims, in the rest of that document—the part few people bother to read today—the authors mainly protested against the British king for violating rights that, with some exaggeration, they had previously enjoyed as Englishmen.

The republican phase. The next phase, creating a popular republic, had begun with the astounding declaration on July 4, 1776, "that all Men are created equal." The Declaration marks the beginning of a series of events that went much further than simply gaining independence from Britain. In what the historian Gordon Wood has called the "greatest Utopian movement in American history,"[21] the Declaration also triggered a democratic revolution in beliefs, practices, and institutions—or better, an evolution—that has continued ever since. The two decades since independence had provided still more, and deeper, experience in the practices of self-government. Nor was this experience limited to a tiny minority. In some of the thirteen states, a fairly high proportion of adult males had acquired the franchise.[22]

Toward a democratic republic. The lengthy colonial and post-independence experience provided a sturdy foundation for the efforts that Americans now undertook in the next phase of the revolution, when the new republic was transformed into a *more democratic republic*. To be sure, at the end of the eighteenth century few Americans were ready to concede that the principles of the Declaration, much less democratic citizenship, applied to everyone.[23] It would take two more centuries of evolution in democratic beliefs before most Americans would be inclined to agree that the famous claim in the Declaration might be rephrased: not just "all men," but "all *persons* are created equal."

Yet always keeping in mind the huge and persistent exceptions, by the standards prevailing elsewhere in the world the extent of equality among Americans was extraordinary. Alexis de Tocqueville, who observed Americans during his year's visit in 1831–32, opened his famous work with these words:

> Among the novel objects that attracted my attention during my stay in the United States, nothing struck me more forcibly than the general equality of conditions. I readily discovered the prodigious influence which this primary fact exercises on the whole course of society, by giving a certain direction to public opinion, and a certain tenor to the laws; by imparting new maxims to the governing powers, and peculiar habits to the governed.
>
> I speedily perceived that the influence of this fact extends far beyond the political character and the laws of the country, and that it has no less empire over civil society than over the Government. . . .
>
> The more I advanced in the study of American society, the more I perceived that the equality of condition is the fundamental fact from which all others seem to be derived, and the central point at which all my observations constantly terminated.[24]

During the three decades before Tocqueville arrived, under the leadership of Jefferson, Madison, and others, supporters of a more democratic republic had already made some changes. The seismic shift from the views of the Framers and the Federalists is symbolized by the changing name of the party that won both the presidency and Congress in the election that Jefferson called— as have later historians—the Revolution of 1800. To defeat the Federalists, win the election, and gain control of the new government, Jefferson and Madison had created a political party that they appropriately named the Democratic-Republican Party. By 1832, with Andrew Jackson as its winning candidate, the Democratic-Republican party became the Democratic Party, plain and simple.[25] The name has stuck ever since.

Conservative delegates among the Framers—later the core of the Federalist Party—had feared that if ordinary people were given ready access to power they would bring about policies contrary to the views and interests of the more privileged classes, which, as the conservative delegates viewed their interests, were also the best interests of the country. These conservative fears were soon confirmed. Within a decade the eminent Federalist leaders were pushed aside and the Federal Party became a minority party. A generation later had seen the demise of both the party and its leaders.

If these changes justified some of the pessimism about popular majorities of many of the Framers, their pessimism proved unjustified in another important respect. A substantial number of the Framers believed that they must erect constitutional barriers to popular rule because the people would prove to be an unruly mob, a standing danger to law, to orderly government, and to property rights. Contrary to these pessimistic appraisals, when American citizens were endowed with the rights and opportunities to support demagogues and rabble rousers, they chose instead to support law, orderly government, and property rights. White male Americans were, after all, mainly farmers who owned their own land; or, where farm land was not easily available because most of it had already been occupied, they could count on the ready availability of good farm land farther west—often obtained, to be sure, at the expense of its earlier inhabitants, the Native Americans.

White Americans in vast numbers bought western land and settled down on their own farms. "Two-thirds of the landless white men of Virginia moved West in the 1790s. . . . Between 1800 and 1820, the trans-Appalachian population grew from a third of a million to more than two million."[26] In foreseeing a democratic republic based on a citizen body consisting predominantly of independent farmers, mainly property owners cultivating their own lands, Jefferson reflected the reality of his time.[27] Outside the South, and even in the southern piedmont, a predominant number of American citizens were free farmers who stood to benefit from an orderly government dependent on their votes.

Ordinary citizens also revealed strong beliefs in democratic values and procedures. Presented with the opportunity to do so, they would choose leaders who cultivated democratic values and procedures. Just such an opportunity was soon presented by four acts passed in 1798 by the Federalists, who were alarmed not only by the seemingly subversive activities of France but also by the rapidly growing influence of boisterous, irreverent, and sometimes libelous opponents in the new Republican party. In particular, the Federalists employed one of these new laws, the Sedition Act, in an effort to silence Republican critics. Notable among the fourteen who were prosecuted was a bombastic and somewhat unsavory Republican congressman, the Irish immigrant Mathew Lyon, whose only memorable contribution to American history was his conviction for sedition, which carried a fine of a thousand dollars—a huge amount in those days—and four months in jail.[28] To the Republicans, the Sedition Act was a flagrant violation of the newly adopted First Amendment. After they gained the presidency and control of Congress in the election of 1800, the Sedition Act was allowed to lapse, despite the vigorous efforts of the Federalists.

Democratic Changes to the Framers' Constitution: Amendments

The fate of the Alien and Sedition Acts symbolizes a larger change at work in the country. The democratic revolution, fitful and uncertain though it would forever remain, not only helped to democratize the formal constitution itself by amendments, it generated new democratic political institutions and practices within which the constitutional system would operate.

The constitutional system that has emerged is no longer that of the Framers, nor is it one they had intended to create.

The Bill of Rights.   To be sure, the first ten amendments to the Constitution—the Bill of Rights—cannot be attributed to the democratic revolution that followed the Convention. They resulted instead from demands within the Convention itself by delegates who generally favored a more democratic system than their colleagues could then accept. Among the most influential of these was George Mason, who wrote the Virginia constitution and its Declaration of Rights. Responding to the insistent demands of Mason and several others, as well as to similar voices outside the Convention, Mason's fellow Virginian, James Madison, drafted ten amendments that were ratified in 1789–90 by eleven states, more than a sufficient number for their adoption. (Incidentally, the two laggards, Georgia and Connecticut, finally did come around—but not until 1939!) Thus, for all practical purposes the Bill of Rights was a part of the original constitution. In any case, the amendments have proved to be a veritable cornucopia of expanding rights necessary to a democratic order.[29]

Other Amendments

As I have mentioned, the most profound violation of human rights permitted by the original constitution, *slavery,* was not corrected until the adoption of the

Thirteenth, Fourteenth, and Fifteenth Amendments between 1865 and 1870. In 1909 the Sixteenth Amendment in 1913 gave Congress the power to enact *income taxes*. The *election of U.S. senators* by state legislatures finally gave way to direct election with the adoption of the Seventeenth Amendment in 1913. *Women* were finally guaranteed the right of suffrage in federal and state elections with the passage of the Nineteenth Amendment in 1919. Although the effort to add an Equal Rights Amendment failed, the Fourteenth Amendment was later interpreted to provide a constitutional basis for eliminating *discrimination* against women as well as certain minorities whose members suffered from discriminatory practices. The iniquitous *poll tax* that had continued to bar African Americans from voting in some southern states was finally forbidden in 1964 by the Twenty-Fourth Amendment. Finally, in a move toward a more inclusive electorate, in 1971 the Twenty-Sixth Amendment reduced the *voting age* to eighteen.

In this halting fashion, the democratic revolution belatedly worked its way through the Constitution to overcome the veto power of long-entrenched minorities and to eliminate some of the most flagrantly undemocratic features of the constitution. As Alan Grimes observed some years ago, of the twenty-six (now twenty-seven) amendments to the constitution, "Twenty-one amendments may be said to affirm either the principle of democratic rights or that of democratic processes."[30]

Democratic Changes in
Political Practices and Institutions

The constitution of the Framers was changed not only
by formal amendments. It was also fundamentally altered by political practices and institutions that the
Framers did not foresee, even though they were unavoidable—indeed, highly desirable—in a democratic
republic.

   Political parties. Perhaps the most important of
these was the political party. The Framers feared and
detested factions, a view famously expressed by Madison
in Federalist No. 10.[31] Probably no statement has been
so often cited to explain and justify the checks against
popular majorities that the Framers attempted to build
into the constitution. It is supremely ironic, therefore,
that more than anyone except Jefferson, it was Madison
who helped to create the Republican Party in order to
defeat the Federalists. Although the system would not
settle down for some years, Jefferson and Madison
helped to inaugurate the competitive two-party system
that has pretty much remained in place ever since.

   Which suggests other questions. Despite the claim
of every political party everywhere in the world that it
truly represents the general interest, aren't political
parties really "factions" in Madison's sense? So did the
Framers fail after all to prevent government by factions? And did they succeed only in making it more
difficult for a majority faction to prevail—that is, a
party reflecting the interests of a majority coalition?

Whatever the best answers to these hard questions, it cannot be denied that partisan politics transformed the constitution. Despite their familiarity with the role of the Tories and Whigs in Britain and nascent parties in their own legislatures, the Framers did not fully foresee that in a democratic republic political parties are not only possible, they are also inevitable and desirable. As Jefferson and Madison soon came to realize, without an organized political party to mobilize their voters in the states and their fellow supporters in the Congress, they could not possibly overcome the entrenched political domination of their political adversaries, the Federalists. The democratic rights incorporated in the Bill of Rights made parties possible; the need to compete effectively made them inevitable; the ability to represent citizens who would otherwise not be adequately represented made them desirable.

Today we take for granted that political parties and party competition are essential to representative democracy: we can be pretty sure that a country wholly without competitive parties is a country without democracy. If the Framers had been aware of the central importance of political parties to a democratic republic, would they have designed their constitution differently? They might well have. At the very least they would not have created the absurdity of an electoral college.

The electoral college.   In an outcome the Framers had made possible by their defective design of the electoral college, the election of 1800 produced a tie between Jefferson and his running mate, Aaron Burr.

From the time the final results were known in late December 1800, the deadlock in the electoral college persisted, despite many attempts at persuasion and compromise, until February 17, 1801, when shifts and abstentions by a number of state delegations gave Jefferson the presidency.[32] Ironically, the very institution that the Framers hoped would insulate the election of the president from partisan politics was its first victim. Although a similar fiasco was prevented in the future by the Twelfth Amendment in 1804, even with the amendment the electoral college was converted by partisan politics into nothing more than a rather peculiar and ritualized way of allocating the votes of the states for president and vice president. Yet the electoral college still preserved features that openly violated basic democratic principles: citizens of different states would be unequally represented, and a candidate with the largest number of popular votes might lose the presidency because of a failure to win a majority in the electoral college. That this outcome was more than a theoretical possibility had already occurred three times before it was displayed for all the world to see in the election of 2000. I'll come back to the democratic shortcomings of the electoral college in a later chapter.

The Democratic Revolution: What Madison Learned—and Taught

James Madison arrived in Philadelphia in 1787, a few months past his thirty-sixth birthday. He was already far from a political neophyte, having been elected at the age of twenty-five to the Virginia constitutional convention where, with George Mason, he helped to draft the Virginia Declaration of Rights and the new state constitution. He then became successively a member of the Virginia legislature (though he failed to be reelected because, it was said, he refused to treat the voters to the customary rum punch), a delegate to the Continental Congress, and again a member of the Virginia legislature. In the months before the Constitutional Convention opened, he drafted the outline of the proposal that would be presented in the opening days of the Convention and that would come to be known as the Virginia Plan. (We shall see something of its contents in the next chapter.)

Yet, experienced as he was, like his fellow delegates Madison brought to the Convention limited knowledge of the institutions and practices that a more fully democratized republic would require. Before his death in 1836 at the age of eighty-five, nearly half a century after the Convention, Madison could have looked back on a rich body of experience that would have shaped his constitutional views in many ways.

Following the Convention, he was elected to the U.S. House of Representatives where he drafted and introduced the first ten amendments to the Constitution—the Bill of Rights. With Jefferson he soon became a leader of the opposition to Federalist policies and ideas. As we have seen, they formed and led the opposition party, the Democratic Republicans. After Jefferson's election, Madison became secretary of state. He then succeeded Jefferson in the presidency. By the time he left that office in 1817, his views about democratic political institutions were probably as well informed as those of any person then alive.

However that may be, the Madison of seventy in 1821 was no longer the Madison of thirty-six in 1787. Among other changes, the Madison of 1821 would have trusted popular majorities—American popular majorities, anyway—far more than the Madison of 1787. The mature and experienced Madison of 1821 might therefore have done less to check majority rule and more to facilitate it. Let me offer several pieces of evidence, one from a time early in his awakening to the requirements of a democratic republic, the others from his reflections in old age.

I have already alluded to the first: the basic alteration in his views about "factions," or what the two distinguished historians of Federalism describe as "Madison Revises *The Federalist*."[33] Madison's views in Federalist No. 10, influenced by his reading of David Hume, are cited endlessly: the dangers of factions, the threat from majorities united on principles contrary to the general interest, political parties as at best a necessary evil. But these were not his more mature views.

In January 1792, less than five years after the close of the Convention, Madison begins to publish a series of essays in *The Gazette,* an opposition newspaper published by Philip Freneau. The first is entitled "On Parties." In "every political society," he writes, "parties are unavoidable." To combat their dangers, Madison offers five proposals that might well serve us better in our own time than the anti-majoritarian biases displayed in Federalist No. 10. Whatever dangers political parties may pose can be overcome

"By establishing political equality among all."

"By withholding *unnecessary* opportunities from a few, to increase the inequality of property by an immoderate, and especially unmerited, accumulation of riches."

"By the silent operation of the laws, which, without violating the rights of property, reduce extreme wealth towards a state of mediocrity, and raise extreme indigence toward a state of comfort."

"By abstaining from measures which operate differently on different interests, and particularly favor one interest, at the expense of another."

"By making one party a check on the other, so far as the existence of parties cannot be prevented, nor their views accommodated."[34]

"If this is not the language of reason," he went on to say, "it is that of republicanism."

Nearly thirty years later (around 1821), when he is preparing his notes on the constitutional debates for publication, he records some of his later reflections. As to the right of suffrage, he remarks that his observations at the Convention "do not convey the speaker's [Madison's] more full and matured view of the subject." "The right of suffrage," he now insists, "is a fundamental Article in Republican Constitutions." He also makes explicit his view of political parties: "No free Country," he says, "has ever been without parties, which are a natural offspring of Freedom." But political parties and a broad suffrage may create a conflict over property. "An obvious and permanent division of every people is into the owners of the Soil, and the other inhabitants." Consequently, if the suffrage is extended to citizens who are not freeholders, a majority might threaten the property rights of the freeholders.

Madison then considers a number of possible solutions to this problem, of which the first would be to restrict the suffrage to "freeholders, and to such as hold an equivalent property." He rejects this solution with an observation that might well have been a central principle of the Second Phase of the American Revolution. "The objection to this regulation," he writes, "is obvious. It violates the vital principle of free Govt. that those who are to be bound by laws, ought to have a voice in making them. And the violation wd. be more strikingly unjust as the lawmakers became the minority." A second option is "confining the right of suffrage for one branch to the holders of property, and for the other Branch to those without property." But to do so "wd. not in fact be either equal or fair." Nor prudent: "The division of the State into the two Classes . . . might lead to contests & antipathies not dissimilar to those between the Patricians and Plebeians at Rome."

After examining other possibilities, he concludes:

Under every view of the subject, it seems indispensable that the Mass of Citizens not be without a voice, in making the laws which they are to obey, & in chusing the Magistrates, who are to administer them, and if the only alternative be between an equal & universal right of suffrage for each branch of the Govt. and a confinement of the *entire* right to a part of the Citizens, *it is better that those having the greater interest at stake namely that of property & persons both, should be deprived of half their share in the Govt. than, that those having the lesser interest, that of personal rights only, should be deprived of the whole.*[35]

The older Madison is also more favorable to majority rule. Like most of his contemporaries, Madison believes that "all power in human hands is liable to be abused." But taking that assumption as axiomatic together with the need for government, the relevant question becomes: what kind of government is best? His answer remains unchanged:

> In Governments independent of the people, the rights and views of the whole may be sacrificed to the views of the Government. In Republics, where the people govern themselves, and where, of course, the majority govern, a danger to the minority arises from opportunities tempting a sacrifice of their rights to the interest, real or supposed, of a majority. No form of government, therefore, can be a perfect guard against the abuse of power. The recommendation of the republican form is, that the danger of abuse is less than any other.[36]

What *has* changed is his greater confidence in majority rule. Compared with its alternatives at least, the mature Madison is confident that majority rule, in the words of Marvin Meyers, promises the "least imperfect government."[37]

"[E]very friend to Republican Government," he writes in 1833, "ought to raise his voice against the sweeping denunciation of majority Governments as the most tyrannical and intolerable of all Governments."

> It has been said that all Government is an evil. It would be more proper to say that the necessity of any government is a misfortune. This necessity however exists; and the problem to be solved is, not what form of government is perfect, but which of the forms is least imperfect; and here the general question must be between a republican Government in which the majority rule the minority, and a government in which a lesser number or the least number rule the majority.
>
> The result . . . is, that we must refer to the monitory reflection that no government of human device and human administration can be perfect; that that which is the least imperfect is therefore the best government; that the abuses of all other governments have led to the preference of republican government as the best of all governments, because the least imperfect; that the vital principle of republican government is the *lex majoris parties,* the will of the majority.[38]

★   ★   ★

I HAVE LITTLE DOUBT THAT IF THE AMERICAN CONSTItutional Convention had been held in 1820, a very different constitution would have emerged from the deliberations—although, I hasten to add, we can never know what shape that constitution might have taken. We can be reasonably sure, however, that the delegates would have attempted to provide more support for, and fewer barriers to, a democratic republic.

As to the undemocratic features of the constitution created in 1787, let me suggest four conclusions.

First, the aspects of the constitution that are most defective from a democratic point of view do not necessarily all reflect the intentions of the Framers, insofar as we may surmise them. Though the flaws are traceable to their handiwork, they are in some cases flaws resulting from the inability of these superbly talented craftsmen to foresee how their carefully crafted instrument of government would work under the changing conditions that were to follow—and most of all, under the impact of the democratic revolution in which Americans were, and I hope still are, engaged.

Second, some of the undemocratic aspects of the original design also resulted from the logrolling and compromises that were necessary to achieve agreement. The Framers were not philosophers searching for a description of an ideal system. Nor—and we may be forever grateful to them for this—were they philosopher kings entrusted with the power to rule. They were practical men, eager to achieve a stronger national government, and as practical men they made compromises. Would the country have been better off if they had refused to do so? I doubt it. But in any case, they did compromise, and even today the constitution bears the results of some of their concessions.

I'll have more to say on that point in my next chapter.

Third, undemocratic aspects that were more or less deliberately built into the constitution overestimated the dangers of popular majorities—American popular majorities, at any rate—and underestimated the strength of the developing democratic commitment among Americans. As a result, in order to adapt the original framework more closely to the requirements of the emerging democratic republic, with the passage of time some of these aspects of the original constitution were changed, sometimes by amendment, sometimes, as with political parties, by new institutions and practices.

Finally, though the defects seem to me serious and may grow even more serious with time, Americans are not much predisposed to consider another constitution, nor is it clear what alternative arrangements would serve them better.

As a result, the beliefs of Americans in the legitimacy of their constitution will remain, I think, in constant tension with their beliefs in the legitimacy of democracy.

For my part, I believe that the legitimacy of the constitution ought to derive solely from its utility as an instrument of democratic government—nothing more, nothing less. In my last chapter, I'll reflect further on the meaning of that judgment.

CHAPTER 3

The Constitution as a Model: An American Illusion

M ANY AMERICANS APPEAR TO BELIEVE THAT OUR constitution has been a model for the rest of the democratic world.[1] Yet among the countries most comparable to the United States and where democratic institutions have long existed without breakdown, not one has adopted our American constitutional system. It would be fair to say that without a single exception they have all rejected it. Why?

Before I explore that question, I need to clarify two matters. As you may have noticed, rather than speaking simply of "the constitution," I've sometimes used the phrase "the constitutional system." I do so because I want to include in a constitutional *system* an important set of institutions that may or may not be prescribed in the *formal* constitution itself: these are its electoral arrangements. As we'll see, electoral systems can interact in crucial ways with the other political institutions and thereby determine the way they function.

Also, I've just referred to the countries where democracy is oldest and most firmly established. We could call them the older democracies, the mature democracies, the stable democratic countries, and so on, but I'll settle on "the advanced democratic countries." Whatever we choose to call them, in order to compare the characteristics and performance of the American constitutional system with the characteristics and performance of the systems in other democratic countries, we need a set of reasonably comparable democratic countries. In short, we don't want to compare apples and oranges—or good apples and rotten apples.

I've noticed that we Americans often assure ourselves of the superiority of our American political system by comparing it with political systems in countries ruled by nondemocratic regimes or in countries that suffer from violent conflict, chronic corruption, frequent chaos, regime collapse or overthrow, and the like. On voicing or hearing criticism of political life in the United States, an American not infrequently adds, "Yes, but just compare it with X!," a favorite X being the Soviet Union during the Cold War and, after its collapse, Russia. One could easily pick more than a hundred other countries with political systems that by almost any standard are unquestionably inferior to our own. But comparisons like this are absurdly irrelevant.

To my mind, the most comparable countries are those in which the basic democratic political institutions have functioned without interruption for a fairly long time, let's say at least half a century, that is, since 1950. Including the United States, there are twenty-two such countries in the world.[2] (See Appendix B, Tables 1 and 2.) Fortunately for our purposes, they are also comparable in their relevant social and economic conditions: not a rotten apple in the bunch. Not surprisingly, they are mostly European or English speaking, with a few outliers: Costa Rica, the only Latin American country; Israel, the only Middle Eastern country; and Japan, the only Asian country.

When we examine some of the basic elements in the constitutional structures of the advanced democratic countries, we can see just how unusual the American system is. Indeed, among the twenty-two older democracies, our system is unique.[3]

Federal or Unitary

To begin with, among the other twenty-one countries we find only seven federal systems, in which territorial units—states, cantons, provinces, regions, Länder—are endowed by constitutional prescription and practice with a substantial degree of autonomy and with significant powers to enact legislation. As in the United States, in these federal countries the basic territorial units, whether states, provinces, or cantons, are not simply legal creatures of the central government with boundaries and powers that the central government could, in principle, modify as it chooses. They are basic elements in the constitutional design and in the political life of the country.

As with the United States, so too in these other five countries federalism was not so much a free choice as a self-evident necessity imposed by history. In most, the federal units—states, provinces, cantons—existed before the national government was fully democratized. In the extreme case, Switzerland, the constituent units were already in place before the Swiss Confederation itself was formed from three Alpine cantons in 1291, five centuries before America was born. Throughout the following seven centuries the Swiss cantons, now twenty in number,[4] have retained a robust distinctiveness and autonomy. In the outlier, Belgium, federalism followed long after a unitary government had been imposed on its diverse regional groups. As the brilliant period of Flemish painting, weaving, commerce, and prosperity in the sixteenth and seventeenth centuries reminds us, profound territorial, linguistic, religious, and cultural differences between the predominantly Flemish and Walloon areas existed long before Belgium itself became an independent country in 1830. Despite the persistent cleavages between the Flemish and Walloons, however, federalism did not arrive until 1993 when the three regions—Wallonia, Flanders, and Brussels—were finally given constitutional status. I should point out that the deep divisions between Walloons and Flemish continue to threaten the survival of Belgium as a single country.

The second and third features follow directly from the existence of federalism.

Strong Bicameralism

A natural, if not strictly necessary, consequence of federalism is a second chamber that provides special representation for the federal units. To be sure, unitary systems may also have, and historically all have had, a second chamber. However, in a democratic country with a unitary system, the functions of a second chamber are far from obvious. The question that was posed during the American constitutional convention is bound to arise: Exactly whom or whose interests is a second chamber supposed to represent? And just as the Framers could provide no rationally convincing answer, so too as democratic beliefs grow stronger in democratic countries with unitary governments, the standard answers become less persuasive—in fact, so unpersuasive to the people of the three Scandinavian countries that they have all abolished their second chambers. Like the state of Nebraska, Norway, Sweden, and Denmark also seem to do quite nicely without them. Even in Britain, the gradual advance of democratic beliefs created an inexorable force opposed to the historical powers of the House of Lords. As early as 1911 the Liberals wiped out the power of the Lords to veto "money bills" passed by the Commons. The continuing advance of democratic beliefs during the past century led in 1999 to the abolition of all but ninety-two hereditary seats, whose occupants would be elected by hereditary peers.[5] The future of that ancient chamber remains in considerable doubt.

By the end of the twentieth century, then, a strongly bicameral legislature continued to exist in only four of the advanced democratic countries, all of them federal: in addition to the United States, these were Australia, Germany, and Switzerland. Their existence poses a question: What functions can and should a second chamber perform in a democratic country? And in order to perform its proper functions, if any, how should a second chamber be composed? As the deliberations of the Parliamentary Commission on the future of the House of Lords indicate, these questions admit of no easy answer. It would not be surprising, then, if Britain ends up with no real second chamber at all, even if a ghostly shade of the upper house persists.

Unequal Representation

A third characteristic of federal systems is significant unequal representation in the second chamber. By unequal representation I mean that the number of members of the second chamber coming from a federal unit such as a state or province is not proportional to its population, to the number of adult citizens, or to the number of eligible voters. The main reason, perhaps the only real reason, why second chambers exist in all federal systems is to preserve and protect *unequal* representation. That is, they exist primarily to ensure that the representatives of small units cannot be readily outvoted by the representatives of large units. In a word, they are designed to construct a barrier to majority rule at the national level.

To make this clear, let me extend the range of the term unequal representation to include any system where, in contrast to the principle of "one person one vote," the votes of different persons are given unequal weights. Whenever the suffrage is denied to some persons within a system, we might say that their votes are counted as zero, whereas the votes of the eligible citizens are counted as one. When women were denied the vote, a man's vote effectively counted for one, a woman's for nothing, zero. When property requirements were required for the suffrage, property owners were represented in the legislature, those below the property threshold were not: like women their "votes" counted for zero. Some privileged members of Parliament, like Edmund Burke, referred to "virtual representation," where the aristocratic minority represented the best interests of the entire country. But the bulk of the people who were excluded easily saw through that convenient fiction, and as soon as they were able to they rejected these pretensions and gained the right to vote for their own M.P.s. In nineteenth-century Prussia, voters were divided into three classes according to the amount of their property taxes. Because each *class* of property owners was given an equal number of votes irrespective of the vast difference in numbers of *persons* in each class, a wealthy Prussian citizen possessed a vote that was effectively worth almost twenty times that of a Prussian worker.[6]

To return now to the United States: as the American democratic credo continued episodically to exert its effects on political life, the most blatant forms of unequal representation were in due time rejected. Yet, one monumental though largely unnoticed form of unequal representation continues today and may well continue indefinitely. This results from the famous Connecticut Compromise that guarantees two senators from each state.

Imagine a situation in which your vote for your representative is counted as one while the vote of a friend in a neighboring town is counted as seventeen. Suppose that for some reason you and your friend each change your job and your residence. As a result of your new job, you move to your friend's town. For the same reason, your friend moves to your town. Presto! To your immense gratification you now discover that simply by moving, you have acquired sixteen more votes. Your friend, however, has lost sixteen votes. Pretty ridiculous, is it not?

Yet that is about what would happen if you lived on the western shore of Lake Tahoe in California and moved less than fifty miles east to Carson City, Nevada,

while a friend in Carson City moved to your commu-
nity on Lake Tahoe. As we all know, both states are
equally represented in the U.S. Senate. With a population in 2000 of nearly 34 million, California had two
senators. But so did Nevada, with only 2 million residents. Because the votes of U.S. senators are counted
equally, in 2000 the vote of a Nevada resident for the
U.S. Senate was, in effect, worth about seventeen times
the vote of a California resident. A Californian who
moved to Alaska might lose some points on climate,
but she would stand to gain a vote worth about fifty-
four times as much as her vote in California.[7] Whether
the trade-off would be worth the move is not for me
to say. But surely the inequality in representation it
reveals is a profound violation of the democratic idea
of political equality among all citizens.

Some degree of unequal representation also exists
in the other federal systems. Yet the degree of unequal
representation in the U.S. Senate is by far the most
extreme. In fact, among all federal systems, including
those in more newly democratized countries—a total
of twelve countries—on one measure the degree of
unequal representation in the U.S. Senate is exceeded
only by that in Brazil and Argentina.[8]

Or suppose we take the ratio of representatives in
the upper chamber to the populations of the federal
units. In the United States, for example, the two senators from Connecticut represent a population of slightly
above 3.4 million, while the two senators from its neighbor New York represent a population of 19 million:

a ratio of about 5.6 to 1. In the extreme case, the ratio of over-representation of the least populated state, Wyoming, to the most populous state, California, is just under 70 to 1.[9] By comparison, among the advanced democracies the ratio runs from 1.5 to 1 in Austria to 40 to 1 in Switzerland. In fact, the U.S. disproportion is exceeded only in Brazil, Argentina, and Russia.[10]

On what possible grounds can we justify this extraordinary inequality in the worth of the suffrage?

A brief digression: rights and interests.   A common response is to say that people in states with smaller populations need to be protected from federal laws passed by congressional majorities that would violate their basic rights and interests. Because the people in states like Nevada or Alaska are a geographical minority, you might argue, they need to be protected from the harmful actions of national majorities. But this response immediately raises a fundamental question. *Is there a principle of general applicability that justifies an entitlement to extra representation for some individuals or groups?*

In searching for an answer, we need to begin with an eternal and elementary problem in any governmental unit:[11] whether the unit is a country, state, municipality, or whatever, virtually all of its decisions will involve some conflict of interests among the people of the relevant political unit. Inevitably, almost any governmental decision will favor the interests of some citizens and harm the interests of others. The solution to this problem, which is inherent in all governmental units, is ordinarily provided in a democratic system by the need to secure a fairly broad consent for its decisions by means, among other things, of some form of majority rule. Yet if decisions are arrived at by majority rule, then the possibility exists, as Madison and many others have observed, that the interests of *any* minority will be damaged by a majority. Sometimes, fortunately, mutually beneficial compromises may be found. But if the interests of a majority clash irreconcilably with those of a minority, then the interests of that minority are likely to be harmed.

Some interests, however, may be protected from the ordinary operation of majority rule. To a greater or lesser degree, all democratic constitutions do so.

Consider the protections that all Americans enjoy, not just in principle but substantially in practice as well. First, the Bill of Rights and subsequent amendments provide a constitutional guarantee that certain fundamental rights are protected whether a citizen lives in Nevada or California, Rhode Island or Massachusetts, Delaware or Pennsylvania. Second, an immense body of federal law and judicial interpretation based on constitutional provisions enormously extends the domain of protected rights—probably far beyond anything the Framers could have foreseen. Third, the constitutional division of powers in our federal system provides every state with an exclusive or overlapping domain of authority on which a state may draw in order to extend even further the protections for the particular interests of the citizens of that state.

The basic question. Beyond these fundamental and protected rights and interests, do people in the smaller states possess *additional* rights or interests that are entitled to protection from policies supported by national majorities? If so, what are they? And on what general principle can their special protection be justified? Surely they do not include a fundamental right to graze sheep or cattle in national forests or to extract minerals from public lands on terms that were set more than a century ago. Why should geographical location endow a citizen or group with special rights and interests, above and beyond those I just indicated, that should be given additional constitutional protection?

If these questions leave me baffled, I find myself in good company. "Can we forget for whom we are forming a government?" James Wilson asked at the Constitutional Convention. "Is it for *men,* or for the imaginary beings called *States?*" Madison was equally dubious about the need to protect the interests of people in the small states. " Experience," he said, "suggests no such danger. . . . Experience rather taught a contrary lesson. . . . The states were divided into different interests not by their differences in size, but by other circumstances."[12]

Two centuries of experience since Madison's time have confirmed his judgment. Unequal representation in the Senate has unquestionably failed to protect the fundamental interests of the *least* privileged minorities. On the contrary, unequal representation has sometimes served to protect the interests of the *most* privileged minorities. An obvious case is the protection of the rights of slaveholders rather than the rights of their slaves. Unequal representation in the Senate gave absolutely no protection to the interests of slaves. On the contrary, throughout the entire pre–Civil War period unequal representation helped to protect the interests of slave owners. Until the 1850s equal representation in the Senate, as Barry Weingast has pointed out, gave the "the South a veto over any policy affecting slavery." Between 1800 and 1860 eight anti-slavery measures passed the House, and all were killed in the Senate.[13] Nor did the Southern veto end with the Civil War. After the Civil War, Senators from elsewhere were compelled to accommodate to the Southern veto in order to secure the adoption of their own policies. In this way the Southern veto not only helped to bring about the end of Reconstruction; for another century it prevented the country from enacting federal laws to protect the most basic human rights of African Americans.

So much for the alleged virtues of unequal representation in the Senate.

Suppose for a moment we try to imagine that we actually wanted the constitution to provide special protection to otherwise disadvantaged minorities by giving them extra representation in the Senate. What minorities most need this extra protection? How would we achieve it? Would we now choose to treat certain states as minorities in special need of protection simply because of their smaller populations? Why would we want to protect these regional minorities and not other, far weaker minorities? To rephrase James Wilson's question in 1787: Should a democratic government be designed to serve the interests of "the imaginary beings called States," or should it be designed instead to serve the interests of all its citizens considered as political equals?

As I have said, the United States stands out among twenty-two comparable democratic countries for the degree of unequal representation in its upper chamber. Of the half dozen that have federal systems and an upper house designed to represent the federal units, none come even close to the United States in the extent of its unequal representation in its upper house.

We begin to see, then, that our constitutional system is unusual. As we continue our exploration we shall discover that it is not merely unusual. It is one of a kind.

Strong Judicial Review of National Legislation

Not surprisingly, other federal systems among the older democracies also authorize their highest national courts to strike down legislation or administrative actions by the federal units—states, provinces, and the like—that are contrary to the national constitution. The case for the power of federal courts to review state actions in order to maintain a federal system seems to me straightforward, and I accept it here. But the authority of a high court to declare unconstitutional legislation that has been properly enacted by the coordinate constitutional bodies—the parliament or in our system the Congress and the president—is far more controversial.

If a law has been properly passed by the law-making branches of a democratic government, why should judges have the power to declare it unconstitutional? If you could simply match the intentions and words of the law against the words of the constitution, perhaps a stronger case could be made for judicial review. But in all important and highly contested cases, that is simply impossible. Inevitably, in interpreting the constitution judges bring their own ideology, biases, and preferences to bear. American legal scholars have struggled for generations to provide a satisfactory rationale for the extensive power of judicial review that has been wielded by our Supreme Court. But the contradiction remains between imbuing an unelected body—or in the American case, five out of nine justices on the Supreme Court—with the power to make policy decisions that affect the lives and welfare of millions of Americans. How, if at all, can judicial review be justified in a democratic order? I'll discuss that question in my last chapter.

Meanwhile, let me return to another aberrant aspect of the American constitutional system.

Electoral Systems

Earlier I explained that I wanted to use the term constitutional *system* because some arrangements that are not necessarily specified in a country's constitutional document interact so strongly with the other institutions that we can usefully regard them as a part of the country's constitutional arrangements. In that spirit, we might want to reflect on the peculiarities of our electoral system, which, natural as it may seem to us, is of a species rare to the vanishing point among the advanced democratic countries. Closely allied with it is an equally rare bird, our much revered two-party system.

To be sure, our electoral system was not the doing of the Framers, at least directly, for it was shaped less by them than by British tradition. The Framers simply left the whole matter to the states and Congress,[14] both of which supported the only system they knew, one that had pretty much prevailed in Britain, in the colonies, and in the newly independent states.

The subject of electoral systems is fearfully complex and for many people fearfully dull as well. I shall therefore employ a drastic oversimplification, but one sufficient for our purposes. Let me simply divide electoral systems into two broad types, each with a variant or two. In the one we know best, typically you can cast your vote for only one of the competing candidates, and the candidate with the most votes wins. In the usual case, then, a single candidate wins office by gaining at least one more vote than any of his or her opponents. We Americans tend to call this one-vote margin a plurality; elsewhere, to distinguish it from an absolute majority it may be called a relative majority. To describe our system, American political scientists sometimes employ the cumbersome expression "single member district system with plurality elections." I prefer the British usage: on the analogy of a horse race where the winner needs only a fraction of a nose-length to win, the British tend to call it the "first-past-the-post" system.

If voters were to cast their ballots in the same proportion in every district, the party with the most votes would win every seat. In practice, as a result of variations from district to district in support for candidates, a second party generally manages to gain some seats, although its percentage of seats will ordinarily be smaller than its percentage of votes. But the representation of third parties usually diminishes to the vanishing point. In short, first-past-the-post favors two-party systems.

The main alternative to first-past-the-post is proportional representation. As the name implies, proportional representation is designed to ensure that voters in a minority larger than some minimal size—say, 5 percent of all voters—will be represented more or less in proportion to their numbers. For example, a group consisting of 20 percent of all voters might win pretty close to 20 percent of the seats in the parliament. Consequently, countries with proportional representation systems are also very likely to have multiparty systems in which three, four, or more parties are represented in the legislature. In short, although the relationship is somewhat imperfect, in general a country with first-past-the-post is likely to have a two-party system and a country with proportional representation is likely to have a multiparty system.

In the most common system of proportional representation, each party presents voters with a list of its candidates; voters cast their votes for a party's candidates; each party is then awarded a number of seats roughly in proportion to its overall share of the vote. Countries with a list system may also permit voters to indicate their preferences among the party's candidates. The party's seats are then filled by the candidates who are most preferred by the voters. Twelve of the twenty-two advanced democratic countries employ the list system of proportional representation, and another six use some variant of it. (See Appendix B, Table 3.)

Of the four countries without proportional representation, France avoids one of the defects of single-member districts by providing that in parliamentary districts where no candidate receives an absolute majority of votes, a second election will be held in which the two candidates with the highest number of votes compete. This run-off, two-round, or double-ballot system, as it is variously called, thereby ensures that all the members have been elected by a majority of the voters in their constituency.

This leaves the three oddballs with first-past-the-post, a plurality system in single member districts: Canada, the United Kingdom, and the United States. Even in the United Kingdom, the original source on which the Americans drew, the traditional system was replaced by proportional representation in the 1999 elections to the newly created legislative bodies in Scotland and Wales. Four parties won seats in the Scottish Parliament, and four too in the Welsh Assembly. What is more, the Independent Commission on the Voting System set up by the Labor Party in 1997 to recommend an alternative to first-past-the-post proposed in its report a year later that members of the House of Commons be elected by means of a proportional representation system—a hybrid, to be sure, but one that would ensure greater proportionality between votes and seats in that ancient house.[15] It is altogether possible that one day not far off, Britain will be added to the list of proportional representation countries, leaving only Canada and the United States among the advanced democracies with first-past-the-post.

Although few Americans know much about experience in the other advanced democratic countries with proportional representation and multiparty systems, they seem to have strong prejudices against both. Unwilling to conceive of an alternative to first-past-the-post and under pressure to ensure fairer representation for minorities in state legislatures and Congress, our legislatures and federal courts in recent years have sometimes gerrymandered weirdly shaped districts. . . well, yes, rather like a salamander. But neither legislatures nor courts seem willing to give serious thought to some form of proportional representation as quite possibly a better alternative.

The extent to which we take first-past-the-post for granted was clearly revealed in 1993, when it was discovered that a well-qualified candidate to head the Civil Rights Division of the Department of Justice had written an article in a law journal suggesting that a rather sensible system of proportional representation might be worth considering as a possible solution to the problem of securing more adequate minority representation.[16] From the comments the author's innocent heresy generated, you might have thought that she had burned the American flag on the steps of the Supreme Court. Her candidacy, naturally, was stone dead.

First-past-the-post was the only game in town in 1787 and for some generations thereafter. Like the locomotive, proportional representation had not yet been invented. It was not fully conceived until the mid-nineteenth century when a Dane and two Englishmen—one of them John Stuart Mill—provided a systematic formulation. Since then it has become the system overwhelmingly preferred in the older democracies.

After more than a century of experience with other alternatives, isn't it time at last to open our minds to the possibility that first-past-the-post may be just fine for horse races but might not be best for elections in a large and diverse democratic country like ours? Might we not also want to consider the possible advantages of a multiparty system?

I do not say that we should necessarily make these choices. But should we not at least give them serious consideration? Shouldn't we ask ourselves this question: What kind of electoral and party systems would best serve democratic ends?

Party Systems

Nearly a half-century ago, a French political scientist, Maurice Duverger, proposed what came to be called Duverger's Law: first-past-the-post electoral systems tend to result in two-party systems. Conversely, proportional representation systems are likely to produce multiparty systems.[17] Although the causal relation may be more complex than my brief statement of Duverger's Law suggests,[18] a country with a proportional representation system is likely to require coalition governments consisting of two or more parties. In a country with a first-past-the-post electoral system, however, a single party is more likely to control both the executive and the legislature. Thus in countries with proportional representation–multiparty systems and coalition governments, minorities tend to be represented more effectively in governing. By contrast, in countries with first-past-the-post and two-party systems, the government is more likely to be in the hands of a single party that has gained a majority of seats in the parliament and the most popular votes, whether by an outright majority, or more commonly, a plurality. To distinguish the two major alternatives, I'll refer to the proportional representation–multiparty countries as "proportional" and countries with first-past-the-post electoral systems and only two major parties as "majoritarian."[19]

Where does the United States fit in? As usual: in neither category. It is a mixed system, a hybrid, neither predominantly proportional nor predominantly majoritarian. (See Appendix B, Table 4.) I am going to return to the American hybrid in Chapter 5, but three brief observations may help to put it in perspective here. First, the Framers had no way of knowing about the major alternatives to first-past-the-post, much less fully understanding them. Second, since the Framers' time most of the older and highly stable democratic countries have rejected first-past-the-post and opted instead for proportional systems. Third, our mixed design contributes even further to the unusual structure of our constitutional system.

Our Unique Presidential System

As we make our way through the list of countries that share some constitutional features with the United States, the list, short to begin with, diminishes even further. By the time we reach the presidency the United States ceases to be simply unusual. It becomes unique.

Among the twenty-two advanced democracies, the United States stands almost alone in possessing a single popularly elected chief executive endowed with important constitutional powers—a presidential system. Except for Costa Rica, all the other countries govern themselves with some variation of a parliamentary system in which the executive, a prime minister, is chosen by the national legislature. In the mixed systems of France and Finland, most of the important constitutional powers are assigned to the prime minister, but an elected president is also provided with certain powers—chiefly over foreign relations. This arrangement may lead, as in France, to a president from one major party and a prime minister from the opposing party, a situation that with a nice Gallic touch the French call "cohabitation." Yet even allowing for the French and Finnish variations, none of the other advanced democratic countries has a presidential system like ours.

Why is this? The question breaks down into several parts. Why *did* the Framers choose a presidential system? Why *didn't* they choose a parliamentary system? Why have all the other advanced democratic countries rejected our presidential system? Why have they adopted some variant of a parliamentary system instead, or as in France and Finland a system that is predominantly parliamentary with an added touch of presidentialism?

To answer these questions in detail would go beyond our limits here. But let me sketch a brief answer.

Before I do so, however, I want to admonish you not to cite the explanation given in the Federalist Papers. These were very far from critical, objective analyses of the constitution. If we employ a dictionary definition of propaganda as "information or ideas methodically spread to promote or injure a cause, nation, etc.," then the Federalist Papers were surely propaganda. They were written post hoc by partisans— Alexander Hamilton, John Jay, and James Madison— who wanted to persuade doubters of the virtues of the proposed constitution in order to secure its adoption in the forthcoming state conventions. Although they were very fine essays indeed, and for the most part much worth reading today, they render the work of the convention more coherent, rational, and compelling than it really was. Ironically, by the way, the task of explaining and defending the Framers' design for the presidency was assigned to Hamilton, who had somewhat injudiciously remarked in the Convention that as to the executive, "The English model was the only good one on this subject," because "the hereditary interest of the king was so interwoven with that of the nation. . . and at the same time was both sufficiently independent and sufficiently controuled [*sic*], to answer the purpose." He then proposed that the executive and one branch of the legislature "hold their places for life, or at least during good behavior."[20] Perhaps as a result of these remarks, Hamilton seems to have had only a modest influence in the Convention on that matter or any other.

How it came about.   What is revealed in the most complete record of the Convention[21] is a body floundering in its attempts to answer an impossibly difficult question: How should the chief executive of a republic be selected, and what constitutional powers should be assigned to the executive branch? The question was impossibly difficult because, as I emphasized in the previous chapter, the Framers had no relevant model of republican government to give them guidance. Most of all, they lacked any suitable model for the executive branch. To be sure, they could draw on the sacred doctrine of "separation of powers." Not surprisingly, the references to that doctrine recorded in Madison's notes were all positive. And up to a point, its implications were obvious: a republic would need an independent judiciary, a bicameral legislature consisting of a popular house and some kind of second chamber to check the popular house, and an independent executive.

But how was the independent executive to be chosen? How independent of the legislature and of the people should he be? How long should his term of office be? ("He" is, of course, the language of Article II and, like most Americans until recently, the only way the Framers could conceive of the office.) The British constitution was a helpful model for the Framers in some respects. But as a solution to the problem of the executive, it utterly failed them. Despite the respect of the delegates for many aspects of the British constitution, a monarchy was simply out of the question.[22]

Even so, they might have chosen a democratic version of the parliamentary system, as the other evolving European democracies were to do. Although they were unaware of it, even in Britain a parliamentary system was already evolving. Why then didn't the Framers come up with a republican version of a parliamentary system?

Well, they almost did. It has been too little emphasized, I think, that the Framers actually came very
close to adopting something like a parliamentary system. What is more, it is far from clear, to me at least,
why they rejected it and ended up instead with a presidential system.[23] One obvious solution—even more
obvious to us today than it would have been in 1787—
was to allow the national legislature to choose the executive. In fact, throughout most of the Convention
this was their favored solution. Right off the bat on
June 2, only two weeks after the Convention opened,
the Virginia delegation, which contained some of the
best minds and most influential delegates, proposed
that the national executive should be chosen by the national legislature. In Madison's notes, the subsequent
course of that proposal and the alternatives to it has
left a fascinating and often mystifying trail.

The meandering trail they pursued, as best I can
reconstruct it, looks something like this.[24] On three
occasions—July 17, July 24, and July 26—the delegates vote for the selection of the president by "the national legislature," the first time by a unanimous vote,
the last by a vote of 6–3. With one exception every
other alternative is defeated by substantial majorities:
in a puzzling detour on July 19, with Massachusetts divided, they vote 6–3 for electors appointed by the
state legislatures. On July 26, their favored solution,
election by the national legislature, is forwarded to a
Committee on Detail. On August 6 the committee duly
reports in favor of election by the national legislature.

On August 24 two other alternatives fail once again. A new committee to consider the issue reports back on September 4. By now the delegates are eager to wind up a convention that has already gone on for three months. In contradiction to the recommendation of the previous committee, however, this one recommends that the executive be chosen by electors appointed by the state legislatures. Two days later, with nine states in favor and only two opposed, the impatient delegates adopt this solution.

Well, not exactly. What they adopt actually states that: "Each state shall appoint, *in such manner as the legislature thereof may direct,* a number of electors, equal to the whole number of Senators and representatives to which the State may be entitled in Congress." Whatever the Framers intend by these words, they will offer a huge opportunity for the democratic phase of the American revolution to democratize the presidency.

Ten days after they agree on this provision, the constitution is signed and the Convention adjourns.

What this strange record suggests to me is a group of baffled and confused men who finally settle on a solution more out of desperation than confidence. As events were soon to show, they had little understanding of how their solution would work out in practice.

So the question remains with no clear answer: Why, finally, did they fail to adopt the solution they had seemed to favor, a president elected by the Congress, a sort of American version of a parliamentary system? The standard answer no doubt has some validity: they feared that the president might be too beholden to Congress. And all the other alternatives seemed to them worse.

Among these alternatives was election by the people, which had been twice rejected overwhelmingly. Yet it was this twice-rejected solution, election by the people, that was quickly adopted de facto during the democratic phase of the American revolution.

How their solution failed. Perhaps in no part of their work did the Framers fail more completely to design a constitution that would prove acceptable to a democratic people. As I have mentioned, their hope for a group of electors who might exercise their independent judgments about the best candidate to fill the office came a cropper following the election of 1800. But as I shall describe in the next chapter, more was still to come. If the election of 1800 first revealed how inappropriate the electoral college was in a democratic order, the presidential election of 2000, two centuries later, dramatized for all the world to witness the conflict between the Framers' constitution and the democratic ideal of political equality.

Ironically, had they adopted the Virginia Plan and placed the choice of the chief executive in the hands of the legislature, as would become the practice in parliamentary systems, the Framers would have put a bit more distance between the people and the president than their solution provided in practice. Here again, in 1787 they could not anticipate a constitutional design that was yet to evolve fully in Britain and, even later, in other countries on the path to democracy.

The continuing democratic revolution would bring about an even more profound change in the presidency. However deftly Jefferson steered the Congress as he rode the tide of the democratic revolution, he never publicly challenged the standard view that the only legitimate representative of the popular will was the Congress, not the president. Nor did any of his successors, Madison, Monroe, John Quincy Adams, lay down such a claim.

Andrew Jackson did just that. In justifying his use of the veto against Congressional majorities, as the only national official who had been elected by *all* the people and not just by a small fraction, as were Senators and Representatives, Jackson insisted that he alone could claim to represent *all* the people. Thus Jackson began what I have called the myth of the presidential mandate: that by winning a majority of popular (and presumably electoral) votes, the president has gained a "mandate" to carry out whatever he had proposed during the campaign.[25] Although he was bitterly attacked for this audacious assertion, which not all later presidents supported, it gained credibility from its reassertion by Lincoln, Cleveland, Theodore Roosevelt, and Wilson and was finally nailed firmly in place by Franklin Roosevelt.

Whatever we may think of the validity of the claim—I am inclined to think it is little more than a myth created to serve the political purposes of ambitious presidents—it is simply one part of a transformation of the presidency in response to democratic ideas and beliefs that has produced an office completely different from the office that the Framers thought they were creating, vague and uncertain as their intentions may have been.

And a good thing, too, you may say. But if you approve of the democratization of the presidency—or, as I would prefer to say, its pseudo-democratization—aren't you suggesting in effect that the constitutional system *should* be altered to meet democratic requirements?

Why other countries became parliamentary democracies. There is still one more reason why the Framers didn't choose a parliamentary system. They had no model to inspire them. One hadn't yet been invented.

The British constitutional system they knew, and in some respects admired, was already on its way to history's attic of abandoned or failed constitutions. Although no one saw it clearly in 1787, even at the time of the Convention the British constitution was undergoing rapid change. Most important, the monarch was swiftly losing the power to impose a prime minister on the parliament. The contrary assumption was gaining strength: that a prime minister must receive a vote of confidence from both houses of parliament, and that he must resign if and whenever he lost their confidence. But this profound change in the British constitution did not become fully manifest until 1832, too late for the Framers to see its possibilities.

In addition, there was the problem of a monarch. How could a country have a parliamentary system without a symbolic head of state who would perform ceremonial functions, symbolize the unity of the country, and help to confer legitimacy on the parliament's choice by anointing him as prime minister? After the evolution of a parliamentary system in Britain, in due time monarchies also helped the Swedes, the Danes, and the Norwegians—and much later Japan and Spain—to move to a parliamentary system that the monarchy helped to legitimize. But in 1787 the full development of parliamentary democracy in countries with a monarchy was still a long way off. For Americans, a monarch, even a ceremonial monarch, was completely out of the question. So why didn't they split the two functions, ceremonial and executive, by creating a titular head of state to serve in the place of a ceremonial monarch, and a chief executive, the equivalent of a prime minister, to whom executive functions would be assigned? Although that arrangement may seem obvious enough to us now, for the Framers in 1787 it was even more distant than the system that was gradually evolving in Britain, the country they knew best. It was not until after 1875 and the installation of the Third Republic in France that the French evolved a solution that would later be adopted in many other democratizing countries: a president elected by the parliament, or in some cases by the people, who serves as formal head of state, and a prime minister chosen by and responsible to the parliament, who serves as the actual chief executive. But for the Framers this invention, which now seems obvious enough to us, was al-

most as far off and about as difficult to imagine, perhaps, as a transcontinental railroad.

Without intending to do so, then, the Framers created a constitutional framework that under the driving
impact of the continuing American Revolution would
develop a presidency radically different from the one
they had in mind. In time American presidents would
gain office by means of popular elections—a solution
the Framers rejected and feared—and by combining
the functions of a head of state with those of a chief
executive the president would be the equivalent of
monarch and prime minister rolled into one.

I can't help wondering whether the presidency
that has emerged is appropriate for a modern democratic country like ours.

★ ★ ★

SO: AMONG THE OLDER DEMOCRACIES OUR CONSTITU-
tional system is not just unusual. It is unique.

Well, you might say, being unique isn't necessarily
bad. Perhaps our constitutional system is better for it.

Better by what standards? Is it more democratic?
Does it perform better in many ways? Or worse?

These questions are by no means easy to answer—
probably impossible to answer with finality. But before
turning to them, we need to take one more look at that
anomalous vestige of the Framers' work, the electoral
college.

CHAPTER 4

Electing the President

O N THE NIGHT OF NOVEMBER 7, 2000, A DRAMA opened in the United States that absorbed the attention of millions of people until the curtain came down six weeks later. The nation was focused once again on an anomalous institution that had originated in the Framers' search for a suitable way to elect the new republic's chief executive. This was the electoral college, by means of which the presidency was won—not for the first time and perhaps not the last—by a candidate with fewer votes than his rival.[1]

As we saw in the previous chapter, the Framers were baffled by how to conceive of the executive in a republic. How should a republican executive be chosen? During the final debates over the electoral college, James Wilson commented: "This subject has greatly divided the House, and will also divide the people out of doors. It is in truth the most difficult of all on which we have had to decide."[2] Three months after the Convention had adjourned, when his memories were still fresh, he made the same observation to his fellow Pennsylvanians who had assembled to ratify the new constitution: "The convention, sir, were perplexed with no part of this plan, so much as with the mode of choosing the president of the United States."[3]

Every solution seemed worse than the rest. The arrangement they finally cobbled together at the last minute was adopted more out of desperation, perhaps, than out of any great confidence in its success. So why did the delegates finally give their approval to the electoral college? Probably the best answer to our question would be: the Framers settled on an electoral college because they had run out of alternatives.

How the Electoral College Came About

We have discussed how during the three summer months the delegates considered and rejected the most obvious possibilities. From the scanty information available, it is possible to add a few more facts.

On August 6, the Committee on Detail brings in a draft of the Constitution that calls for the election of the president by Congress. This proposal finds no takers. As late as August 24, despite mounting pressures to complete their work and adjourn, the delegates vote down every plausible alternative. Even a motion that the president "shall be chosen by electors" fails to gain a majority of votes. Unable to agree, on the last day of August the delegates turn the problem of choosing the president over to yet another committee, this one drawn from each of the eleven state delegations. Four days later the committee offers one of the solutions the delegates had already rejected earlier: "Each State shall appoint in such manner as its Legislature may direct, a number of electors equal to the whole number of Senators and members of the House of Representatives to which the State may be entitled in the Legislature."[4]

The delegates, no doubt weary of their task and eager to finish, find one remaining flaw. The committee has proposed that in case of a tie vote in the electoral college, the choice will be made by the *Senate* from the five highest candidates. Objection! Many delegates believe, it appears, that the competition for the presidency will usually lead to more than two leading candidates—three, four, five, more. If their conjectures are correct, then the election of the president will frequently, perhaps regularly, fall to the Senate, a body they expect to be highly powerful and rather aristocratic. Wilson forcefully puts the case against conferring that power on the Senate. Combining this additional power "with other parts of the plan," he said, he was "obliged to consider the whole as having a dangerous tendency to aristocracy; as throwing a dangerous power into the hands of the Senate."[5] Others agree, and by a lopsided vote the delegates relocate the power in the hands of the more popular branch.

Thus was the electoral college born.

Why the Electoral College?

To return now to our question. Why did the Framers settle on this solution? The usual answer runs like this: they wanted to remove the choice of the President from the hands of popular majorities and to place the responsibility in the hands of a select body of wise, outstanding, and virtuous citizens—as they clearly saw themselves, a cynic might add. The main source of the standard view seems to be the Federalist No. 68, written by Hamilton. "The immediate election should be made by men most capable of analyzing the qualities adapted to the station, and acting under circumstances favorable to deliberation, and to a judicious combination of all the reasons and inducements which were proper to govern their choice."[6] Nothing, of course, could be further from the reality of the electoral college as it swiftly developed. And even Hamilton appears to have misunderstood the mechanics of the electoral college in one respect: He assumed that "the people of each State shall choose . . . [the] electors."[7] But what the Constitution actually provided, as we just saw, was that the power to determine how the electors were to be chosen was assigned to the state legislatures. And most states did not initially assign that responsibility to the people.

The fullest available explanation for the committee's proposal is one offered by Gouverneur Morris, a member (and probably a highly influential member) of the committee, who ran through the now familiar objections to alternative solutions:

> *Congress:* "The danger of intrigue & faction if the appointmt. [sic] Should be made by the Legislature." "No body appeared to be satisfied with an appointment by the Legislature." "The indispensable necessity of making the Executive independent of the Legislature."
>
> *The People:* "Many were anxious [i.e., in fear][8] even for an immediate choice by the people."
>
> *Cabals and Corruption:* "As the Electors would vote at the same time throughout the U.S. and at so great a distance from each other, the great evil of cabal would be avoided. It would be impossible to corrupt them."[9]

Nothing here of Hamilton's later rationalization, though something like it might have been on the minds of some delegates.

Failure

No part of the constitution revealed the flaws in its design more quickly than the provision for the electoral college. Within a dozen years, the election of 1800 had already displayed two of its defects. The more serious at the time, but easily corrected, was the failure of the Framers to distinguish adequately between electing the president and electing the vice-president.[10] At a congressional caucus in May 1800, the Republicans had unanimously agreed on the nominations of Thomas Jefferson as president and Aaron Burr as vice president. But later on in the electoral college, the votes were split among five candidates: Jefferson and Burr tied for president with 73 votes each; of two Federalist candidates, the incumbent, President John Adams, gained 65, and Charles Cotesworth Pinckney, 64; John Jay, the governor of New York, received 1 vote. As the Constitution prescribed, the deadlock was referred to the House. After thirty-six ballots taken over a week's time, Jefferson finally prevailed with the votes of ten of the sixteen states.

What had not been foreseen by the Framers—a tie between the top two candidates—was now made obvious.[11] The solution was equally obvious. The Twelfth Amendment, requiring separate ballots for president and vice president, was swiftly adopted, in time for the election of 1804.[12]

Although this failure in the Framers' design of the electoral college was easily corrected, the other that was clearly revealed by the election of 1800 remained. It remains still. That presidential election shattered whatever hopes the delegates to the Convention may have entertained that the electoral college would serve as an independent body free of the supposed vices of popular election. Party politics—partisan politics, if you will—had transformed the electors into party agents, a role that except for an aberrant member would continue to be played. The privilege of serving as an elector would typically be awarded not to leading citizens willing to express their independent judgments, as the Framers may have assumed, but to party loyalists, and usually minor ones at that. Thus the development of political parties and party loyalties turned the elaborate machinery of the electoral college into little more than a way of counting votes.

What is more, in a change that I'll come back to in a moment, the democratizing phase of the American revolution speedily put the choice of the president where the Framers had explicitly refused to lodge it: in the hands of the people (that is, the white male voters).

So endeth the aristocratic pretensions of the electoral college.

Inherent Democratic Defects

Even when the electors were chosen by popular election, however, three undemocratic features remained inherent features of the electoral college.

Popular votes versus electoral votes.   First, the candidate with the greatest number of popular votes—a plurality or even an outright majority—might not receive a majority of electoral votes and thus might fail to be chosen president. Four presidential elections—including that of 2000—have led to just such an outcome. In the most famous instance, the election of 1876, a candidate with an outright *majority* of popular votes lost the presidency. The crisis began when Samuel J. Tilden, the Democratic candidate, won 51 percent of the popular votes and yet failed to gain a clear and uncontested majority of votes in the electoral college against his Republican opponent, Rutherford B. Hayes. In the complex political shenanigans that ensued,[13] Southern Democrats in Congress extorted from Hayes a promise to withdraw federal troops from the South, and they promised in turn to respect Negro rights (which, needless to say, they never did). Hayes was then awarded 185 electoral votes to Tilden's 184. In the words of one account: "The country acquiesced. Thus ended a crisis that could have resulted in civil war."[14]

In an additional three elections in which the winning candidate gained fewer popular votes than his rival, *none of the candidates* gained a majority of popular votes. In these cases, which include the election of 2000, the votes cast for third party candidates deprived both major party candidates of a popular majority.[15]

Winning with a minority of popular votes.   In fact, winning the presidency with only a minority of popular votes has been a fairly common occurrence. In a total of eighteen elections, candidates have gained the presidency without winning a majority of popular votes. (See Appendix B, Figure 1.) Overall, then, in one out of every three presidential elections the highest office in the land has been awarded to a candidate chosen by a minority of voters. In a close election where third party candidates pick up some votes, as in the election of 2000, this outcome is highly probable.

Losing though preferred by a majority.   In some cases where no candidate receives a majority of popular votes, if voters' second choices had been taken into account (as they can be in some electoral systems), or if a run-off had occurred between the two highest candidates, it is altogether possible that the outcome might have gone the other way. If voters had been provided with an opportunity to express their second choices in the contested election of 2000, most votes of the major third party candidate, Ralph Nader, would likely have gone to Vice President Gore, in which case Gore would have gained the presidency.

Unequal representation of voters.   To these defects in the electoral college we can add yet one more. Because each state is entitled to "a number of electors equal to the whole number of Senators and Representatives" from that state, unequal representation in the Senate plays itself out once again. Although the effects are somewhat diluted by the inclusion of Representatives in the total, the inequality in the weight of votes in the electoral college is still strong. The vote of a Wyoming resident, for example, is worth almost four times the vote of a California resident in the electoral college. Where the number of residents for each elector runs from 165 thousand to a little more than 300 thousand in the ten smallest states, in the ten largest it ranges from 586 thousand in Georgia to 628 thousand in California. The ten smallest states each choose two to three times as many electors as they would if a state's electors were strictly in proportion to its population.[16] (See Appendix B, Figure 2.)

A Remediable Defect: Winner Take All

The democratic deficiencies inherent in the electoral college were compounded by another item that was deliberately tacked on. For the first elections the states experimented with a variety of methods for choosing the electors. An extreme example was Massachusetts, which "altered its system of selecting electors no fewer than seven times in the first ten presidential elections, often to suit short-term partisan interests."[17] The two major options were to lodge the choice of electors in the legislature or to give the choice to the people; popular choice in turn could be made either in districts—one elector per district—or at large, with the winner taking all the state's electoral votes. Giving the legislature the power to choose the delegates ran sharply contrary to the democratizing currents of the time, and popular election soon predominated. By 1832 only South Carolina continued to lodge the choice with the legislature, a practice it finally abandoned during the Civil War.[18] But of the two systems of popular election, winner-take-all soon predominated as political leaders concluded that by concentrating all the state's electoral votes in a single slate, they could enhance their weight in the electoral college and thus their influence on the elections.

If the winner-take-all system provides some states with strategic advantages in presidential elections, it also has at least three disadvantages. First, it reduces the incentives of a presidential candidate to compete for votes in "safe" states that are clearly going to be taken by one of the two major party candidates. As a consequence, candidates tend to compete most heavily for votes in "swing" states that could reasonably be expected to go either way in the election. Second, it severely reduces the incentives of potential third-party candidates to undertake the costly task of running for president, since they cannot realistically hope to win any votes at all in the electoral college. Finally, for both reasons it may weaken the incentives of many voters in "safe" states to go to the polls: Why bother to vote if you know that a majority of voters in your state will, in effect, choose the entire slate of presidential electors?

Unlike the problems in the electoral college arising from features that are constitutionally prescribed, winner-take-all, as the history of its development clearly demonstrates, can be altered by state legislatures.

Should We Alter It or Abolish It?

In view of its many deficiencies, what should be done with the electoral college? Before turning to that question, let me consider a common objection to changing it. As we saw, the constitutional allocation of electors gives a considerable advantage to a voter in a less populated state and correspondingly reduces the influence of a voter in a larger state. This marked inequality in representation is often defended, as with the more extreme case of the Senate itself, on the ground that the small states *need* and are *entitled* to protection from the large states.

Entitlement. Why should the interests of voters in the small states be entitled to extra protection? The objections I raised in the previous chapter about the Senate are also germane to the electoral college, so I'll repeat them here:

James Wilson at the Constitutional Convention: "Can we forget for whom we are forming a government? Is it for *men* ["persons," we would want to say today] or for the imaginary beings called *States*?"

James Madison: "Experience suggests [that] . . . the states were divided into different interests not by their differences in size, but by other circumstances."

Beyond the protections provided by the Bill of Rights, the constitutional division of powers in our federal system, and an immense body of legislative and judicial protections for basic rights, do people in the less populated states possess *additional* rights or interests that are entitled to special protection by means of unequal representation? If so, specifically what are they?

Is there a *principle of general applicability* that justifies an entitlement to extra representation for some individuals or groups? If so, what is it?

If we were to formulate a general principle and apply it fairly, would not those most entitled to protection be the *least-privileged* minorities—rather than people who happen to live in the smaller states?

I am not aware of any convincing answers to these questions and objections.

Need. Behind the belief that small states need special protection against the larger states may lurk an image of the oversized bully intimidating his weaker fellows. But once again the concrete issue comes down to one of legitimate rights and interests. If the president were elected by popular vote, would the legitimate rights and interests of citizens in the small states suffer from neglect or abuse? The belief that they would suffer rests on the assumption that presidential candidates would have little incentive to compete for the votes of citizens in the small states, and as a result their interests would tend to be neglected in national policy-making.

But this assumption seems to me mistaken. In a system of direct election where every citizen's votes are given equal weight, presidential candidates will be even more eager than they are now to win votes wherever they might be available; and the closer they expect the election to be, the more eagerly they will search out those votes. It is true, of course, that interest groups with many members are likely, as they are with the electoral college, to secure greater consideration than interest groups with few members. But let us imagine two relatively small, similarly sized groups of potential voters, one concentrated in a small state and the other in a large state; both groups, let us assume, possess interests and express demands that are equally compatible with a candidate's general program. Other things being roughly comparable, under a system of popular election the incentives of a presidential candidate to win the votes of the two groups would be equally strong, and the geographical location of each group would be largely irrelevant, conspicuously so in this age of television.

I see no reasonable grounds on which to conclude that the legitimate rights, interests, and demands of voters in small states *should* be privileged or that they would be unjustifiably impaired if the president were popularly elected.

So what *should* we do? And what *can* we do?[19]

What Should We Do About the Electoral College?

From a democratic perspective, the most desirable change would be a constitutional amendment that would replace the electoral college with the direct election of the president by popular vote; if no candidate were to receive more than 50 percent of the popular vote, a run-off election between the top two candidates would be held shortly thereafter.[20]

A second possibility is a constitutional amendment that would maintain the electoral college but require that a state's electoral votes be allocated to candidates in direct proportion to their share of the popular votes in the state.

Finally, even without a constitutional amendment, in response to a ground swell of popular opinion, state legislatures might choose the second solution—and thus return to the district system that, as we saw, was adopted in a number of states in the earliest presidential elections.

What Can We Do?

Evidence from surveys indicates that a substantial majority of Americans would support a reform of the electoral college.[21] In 1989, a proposal to amend the Constitution in order to abolish the electoral college and provide instead for the direct popular election of the president passed the House of Representatives with overwhelming support—338–70, or 83 percent of the votes in the House.[22]

Yet desirable and popular as a reform might be, the most realistic answer to our second question—what can we do?—is: Probably not much. By one count, over seven hundred proposals have been introduced in the House to modify or abolish the electoral college. None have succeeded. As might be expected, the graveyard of constitutional amendments altering the electoral college is the Senate—which, as we have seen, is the citadel of unequal representation. When the proposal for direct election that had passed the House with 83 percent of the votes in 1989 reached the floor of the Senate a year later, it ran into a filibuster—unlimited debate by opponents of a measure they do not want to come to a vote. Under Senate rules, to shut off the debate and get on with the vote would have required the support of 60 Senators—60 percent of the total. The motion to end debate actually did win a majority of votes—54 out of 100; but it failed to gain the 60 percent that the rules required.[23] And even if the proposed amendment had come to a vote, it could not have gained the necessary two-thirds—67 Senators—required for an amendment.

Thus the requirement that an amendment must gain the votes of two-thirds of the members of the Senate gives a veto power to Senators from the small states, and these Senators may act in concert with other colleagues who foresee a reduction in the influence of their states on the presidency.[24]

The relative *desirability* of three possible solutions to the problems of the electoral college appears to be inversely related to the *likelihood* of their enactment. Consequently, however deluded the Framers were about to the way their last-minute improvisation would work in practice, it seems unlikely that we shall manage to erase this undemocratic blemish on the American constitutional system.

★   ★   ★

THE FRAMERS' ATTEMPT TO INSULATE THE CHIEF EX-ecutive from popular choice provides the most telling example of their failure to provide a constitutional system that would be appropriate for a democratic republic. The fate of the electoral college illustrates three aspects of this failure.

First, almost from the beginning the electoral college wholly failed to operate as the Framers had intended. It was, so to speak, swiftly subverted by the emerging democratic forces.

Second, even the more democratized electoral college retained features that could and sometimes did lead to undemocratic outcomes.

Finally, the requirements laid down by the Framers for amending the constitution made it extraordinarily difficult to bring about changes that might be supported by a majority of American citizens.

CHAPTER 5

How Well Does the Constitutional System Perform?

L ET ME REPEAT THE QUESTION I RAISED AT THE beginning: Why should we uphold the American Constitution? One response might be: Because it performs better than any feasible alternative.[1]

If the unique properties of our constitutional system enable it to perform better than the systems of other democratic countries, then it merits our pride and confidence. If these peculiarities don't matter, perhaps we should ignore them. But if it performs worse, then shouldn't we begin to consider possible changes?

Questions about the relative performance of different constitutional systems are easy to pose but extraordinarily difficult to answer responsibly. True, we can find today, as only a generation ago or more we could not, many good indicators of how different countries' systems perform in a variety of important ways: from literacy, education, health, and life expectancy to political and civil rights, incomes, income distribution, and others. It is, however, not easy to determine the extent to which a country's constitutional arrangements influence that country's performance on such matters. As one scientific commonplace puts it: Correlations don't prove causation. If a greater degree of income inequality exists in the United States than in most of our twenty-two established democracies, is this a consequence of our unique constitutional system?

As difficult as questions like this are and although constitution-making is still far from an exact science, we do have more knowledge at our disposal today about different constitutional systems than the Framers could have dreamed of—indeed, more than any generation in history could possibly have assembled. In the years to come we could acquire even better knowledge, if we are determined to do so.

With due respect for uncertainty, then, I want to assess how well our constitutional arrangements perform in comparison with those of the other countries where democracy is well established. I'll use five criteria. To what extent, if at all, do constitutional arrangements help to:

1. maintain the democratic system;
2. protect fundamental democratic rights;
3. ensure democratic fairness among citizens;

4. encourage the formation of a democratic consensus; and
5. provide a democratic government that is effective in solving problems?

Maintaining Democratic Stability

Do different constitutional arrangements significantly affect the chances that a country will preserve its basic democratic institutions—that it will, in short, remain a democracy? This question opens up a vast subject that has been extensively explored in recent years.

Unfortunately for my purposes here, but fortunately for democracy, the experience of our twenty-two democratic countries cannot provide the evidence we need to answer our question about stability. I selected these countries as suitable for comparison with the United States precisely because they are the only countries in the world today that have fully maintained their basic democratic institutions for a half-century or more. Since democratic institutions have never collapsed in any of these countries during that period (or longer), we lack any basis for comparing their performance in maintaining basic democratic stability. For example, if twenty-two persons of greatly varying but moderate diets all remain about equally healthy, we couldn't draw any conclusions about the effects of their diets on their health. So, too, with our twenty-two countries: they have all performed equally well in maintaining the existence of their democratic systems.

From our hypothetical study of diets, however, we could derive one conclusion that is far from trivial: good health is possible within a considerable range of moderate diets. Similarly, from the experience of our twenty-two countries we can draw at least one important conclusion: the differences in their constitutional arrangements evidently have not affected the survival of their basic democratic institutions. Because all of these countries have remained steadily democratic, it follows that within the rather wide range of constitutional variations they exhibit, their differences simply haven't mattered for democratic survival.[2]

How can we explain this surprising conclusion? Let me offer three general propositions.

First, if the conditions in a country are highly favorable for democracy, constitutional differences like those that exist among our twenty-two countries will not affect the stability of the basic democratic institutions. To return to the analogy with diet and health: among a group of people who otherwise live healthy lives, the variations in their moderate diets won't matter much. It would take us too far afield to describe the conditions that favor democratic stability, but we can say that they appear to include such things as the effective control by elected leaders over the military and police, a political culture supportive of democratic beliefs, and a relatively well-functioning economic order, among others.

Although a country with favorable conditions like these is likely to maintain its democratic institutions under a variety of constitutional possibilities, no constitutional system can preserve democracy in a country where these and other favorable conditions are absent. As I said, none of our twenty-two democratic countries have suffered a breakdown of democracy during the past half-century. But if we move back to the previous century, we do find that in one of our countries where all the basic democratic institutions (except for inclusive citizenship) had been in place for more than half a century, the constitutional arrangements could not prevent a breakdown into a civil war—a conflict, moreover, that resulted in vastly greater casualties than the American or the French Revolution. That country was the United States. The conditions necessary for preserving national unity had become so unfavorable that probably no constitutional arrangements could have prevented both secession and civil war. Given the extreme polarization in interests, values, and ways of life between the citizens of the slave states and those of the free states, I cannot imagine *any* democratic constitution under which the two sections could have continued to coexist peacefully in one country.

But suppose that, unlike our twenty-two countries, we have a country in which some conditions are favorable for democracy while others are unfavorable. Might the particular features of a constitution matter in a country where the underlying conditions make democracy rather chancy? It seems possible that in situations of uncertainty, constitutional arrangements might just tip the balance one way or the other, toward democratic stability or democratic breakdown. What does the evidence indicate?

A much debated issue is the effect on democratic stability of presidential versus parliamentary systems. Perhaps because they were impressed by American stability and power, developing countries have often adopted some version of a presidential system. As two scholars have noted, "A remarkable fact . . . is the extent to which presidentialism is a Third World phenomenon."[3] So is the likelihood of breakdown. Are the two connected—presidentialism and breakdown? The answer is a subject of dispute. Some scholars have concluded that in countries where the conditions for a stable democracy are mixed—some favorable, some unfavorable—a presidential system is more likely than a parliamentary system to put a greater strain on democratic survival.[4] Others argue, however, that "parliamentarism has not fared any better in the third world than has presidentialism; arguably, it has fared worse."[5]

To explore this controversial question would take us far outside the purposes of this book, thus I leave it unsettled here but accompanied by four brief admonitions: One, the intricate American constitutional system is probably not suitable for export to other countries. Two, insofar as we Americans can directly influence decisions in newly democratizing countries, we should avoid trying to impose it on them. Three, there is probably no single best constitutional system.

And finally, democratic constitutions need to be tailored to fit the culture, traditions, needs, and possibilities of a particular country.

Protecting Fundamental Rights

If the evidence about democratic stability is inconclusive, what does the evidence show about democratic rights? How well do the constitutional systems of democratic countries protect the rights, opportunities, and duties of both majorities and minorities?

Here we again run into a methodological problem. As I shall explain in more detail in the next chapter, democracy and its fundamental institutions presuppose the existence of certain fundamental rights, such as freedom of speech and freedom of the press. We can reasonably classify all twenty-two of our countries as democratic only because, among other things, they all have maintained a high level of protection for basic democratic rights and liberties. As with stability and breakdown, in selecting our twenty-two countries we have necessarily excluded any in which massive and persistent violations of fundamental political rights have occurred.

Nonetheless, even if we assume that all of them have maintained political rights at or above the basic threshold for democracy, we do find some smaller variations. The important point, however, is that there is no discernible relationship between constitutional systems, broadly defined, and these variations in rights and freedoms. Freedom House, an independent non-profit organization that since 1973 has provided annual evaluations of the conditions of liberty among the countries of the world, assigns the identical score on political rights to all twenty-two democratic countries. On civil liberties, seven countries — Belgium, Costa Rica, France, Germany, Israel, Italy, and the United Kingdom — fall just below the top score.[6] Yet if we go back to our examination of the variations in broad constitutional features that might explain why these seven fall below the rest, none can account for the difference. Federalism, strong bicameralism, unequal representation in the upper house, strong judicial review, the electoral and party systems, and parliamentarism or presidentialism: none provide an explanation. Or consider freedom in print and broadcasting media. At the top, with a near-perfect score in the Freedom House evaluations, is Norway: a nonfederal country with a parliamentary system, a unicameral parliament, proportional representation, multiple parties, coalition governments, and no judicial review of parliamentary enactments. Halfway down, just below the United States, is the Netherlands, another nonfederal country with a parliamentary system, proportional representation, multiple parties, coalition governments, and no judicial review. Why the difference? Or compare four of the federal countries—Switzerland, Australia, the United States, and Germany. Federalism can hardly account for the variations in their scores.[7]

The most relevant conclusion we can draw is that among mature democratic countries, where the conditions for democracy are generally favorable, differences in rights and liberties cannot be attributed to constitutional systems. But if not constitutional systems, then what?

The answer will be found, I believe, in differences in national histories, political cultures, and perceptions of internal and strategic threats to survival. If this is the case, then in the end a democratic country cannot depend on its constitutional systems for the preservation of its liberties. It can depend only on the beliefs and cultures shared by its political, legal, and cultural elites and by the citizens to whom these elites are responsive.

Democratic Fairness

How does the American constitutional system compare with those of other mature democracies in the fairness with which it treats different citizens? As we all know, the question of fairness or justice has been a source of endless debate among the best minds since ancient times. Indeed, differences in views about justice seem to be built into the human condition. I, however, want to bypass these perennial controversies and focus instead on one aspect of fairness that bears directly on the question at hand.

If I may now use the term constitutional system in its broader sense to include electoral arrangements, we can arbitrarily reduce the alternatives to two. In one, which I'll call a proportional system, as a result of proportional representation the percentage of seats won by a party in the legislature will roughly mirror the percentage of votes cast for candidates of that party. In the other, which I'll call a majoritarian system,[8] candidates receiving the most votes in a particular district win that district's single seat, and the other candidates, therefore, win no seats at all. In a proportional system, all minority parties that gain votes above some threshold, such as 5 percent, will be represented in the legislature. In a majoritarian system, if the candidate of one party were to win a plurality (relative majority) of votes in every district, then that party would win *all* the seats. Although such an extreme outcome is only a theoretical possibility, in majoritarian systems the party with a majority of votes does ordinarily win a disproportionately large number of seats; the second largest party gains a disproportionately small number of seats; and all third parties gain few if any seats.

In an earlier chapter I pointed out that proportional representation is likely to produce a multiparty system and coalition governments; first-past-the-post is likely to produce two dominant parties; and in a parliamentary system with two dominant parties, the prime minister and cabinet are likely to be drawn from a single party with a majority of seats, as is typically the case in Britain.

In the debate over the relative desirability of proportionality versus majoritarianism,[9] virtually no one questions that proportionality is fairer to citizens than majoritarianism. Proportionality doesn't necessarily mean, however, that the principle of majority rule entirely stops operating. In the legislature, for example, elected representatives will ordinarily make their decisions by majority rule. But because the governing coalition will generally include representatives from minority parties, governing majorities are likely to be more inclusive than in a majoritarian system. Thus, a proportional system comes closer than a majoritarian system to providing equal representation—an equal say—for all.

Advocates of majoritarianism may concede that proportionality is fairer; but they might argue that a majoritarian system offers two advantages that considerably outweigh its unfairness. For one thing, its defenders often say, proportionality tends to produce governing coalitions that are more unstable and, therefore, more *ineffective* than governments in majoritarian systems. Does the experience of the large number of mature democratic countries with proportional system confirm that their governments are less effective? In a moment I'll turn to evidence bearing on this question. But just suppose we were to find that proportional systems are, in general, no less effective than governments in countries with majoritarian systems. On what grounds could we then reject proportionality?

We might still reject proportionality if we conclude that having two dominant parties rather than the multiplicity of parties typical of proportional systems helps to make governments more *accountable* to voters. Our supposition might run something like this: Two-party majoritarian systems help voters hold governments more accountable because they are better at simplifying and clarifying the alternatives open to voters. Consequently, during campaigns and elections, voters can fix responsibility for the decisions and policies that the government has recently adopted. What is more, because voters in proportional systems face a multiplicity of parties and possible governing coalitions, they may find it difficult to guess what their vote will actually mean. Forming a majority coalition in a multiparty parliament can be a tricky business. If a voter's party wants to be included in the governing coalition, what compromises will it be compelled to make in order to find a place? And what policies will the coalition finally manage to agree on and carry through? In contrast, because voters in majoritarian systems ordinarily have only two realistic choices, they can make more informed guesses about the direction the government is likely to take under one major party or the other.[10]

A justification along these lines would provide strong support for majoritarian systems. But as appealing as it is, the majoritarian vision isn't easily transformed into reality. For one thing, in the small number of countries with nominally majoritarian systems, as Powell points out, we find a "persistent refusal of voters to deliver majority support for a single party or even a preelection coalition." In forty-five elections from 1969 through 1994 in six "predominantly majoritarian" countries, "only in Australia in 1975 and in

France in 1981 did a party or preelection coalition win a clear voter majority." In short, just as happens in American presidential elections, majoritarianism often fails to produce a government that reflects the choices of a majority of voters. Second, the distortion between seats and votes in majoritarian systems sometimes creates a majority of seats for a party that has failed to win even a plurality of votes and thus has actually come in second. In these cases, the minority party among voters becomes the majority party in the legislature. Third, even in majoritarian systems, "in practice, purely two-party politics is a rare phenomenon and often not robust when it appears." That is, a third party—like the Liberal Democrats in Britain—may prevent either of the two major parties from gaining a majority of votes, even though one of them may gain a majority of seats.[11]

Encouraging Consensus

Even if proportionality is fairer than majoritarianism, many Americans will say that the price of fairness is too high. Any country in which multiple parties compete for office, they assume, will surely be divided and contentious and suffer from government by unstable and ineffective coalitions. How valid is this common American view?

In direct contradiction to that view, Arend Lijphart, the scholar who pioneered the comparative analysis of proportionality and majoritarianism in democratic countries, refers to proportional systems as "consensus governments."[12] And rightly so, for experience shows that even if proportionality cannot always overcome deep political, social, cultural, or economic cleavages (as in Israel, for example), a proportional system can sometimes help to maintain internal peace, provide opportunities for compromise among opponents, and produce a broad consensus in favor of not only government policies but the country's political arrangements as well.

Let me offer three examples. In the Netherlands,[13] religious and ideological differences led to a profound division of the country into four basic groups: Protestants, Catholics, Liberals, and Socialists. The four groups became fairly distinctive subcultures pretty much walled off from one another by their own institutions, from newspapers and radio to schools, trade unions, hospitals, marriages, residences, and more. After proportional representation was introduced early in the twentieth century, each of the groups also supported its own separate political party. Not surprisingly, in the late nineteenth and early twentieth centuries these basic cleavages among the four subcultures led to severe conflicts over education, the franchise, and the rights of labor. By 1910 the disputes had became so intense that leaders of the four groups became alarmed for the future of the country. Spurred by their concern, from 1913 to 1917 they not only managed to negotiate acceptable compromises, but they also agreed that the political parties representing the four groups would all be represented in the cabinet. In short, they created a consensus government. Despite the persisting cleavages among the four subcultures, a highly institutionalized system of full inclusion endured for half a century, when demographic changes and a decline in the intensity of the differences reduced the need for complete inclusion of all four parties in every cabinet. Even so, and down to the present day, Dutch governments have continued to emphasize inclusion and consensus rather than majoritarian control of the government.

Or consider Switzerland with its four national languages — German, French, Italian, and the tiny Romansh-speaking population; its two major religions, Protestantism and Catholicism, which were the source of sanguinary conflict until the middle of the nineteenth century; and its two dozen or so cantons, many of which are internally rather homogeneous in language and religion. If you were to reflect on the possibilities of conflict among these subcultures you might conclude that, like the Balkans, Switzerland must be forever bubbling over with intense disputes and might even be on the verge of national disintegration. But the pragmatism, common sense, and national attachments of the Swiss enabled them in 1959 to create a proportional system in which representatives of the four major parties representing the different subcultures are usually all included in the executive branch—the federal council or *Bundesrat*.

It is a reasonable conclusion that majoritarian systems in Switzerland and in the Netherlands would have made the search for governments based on a broad consensus among different subcultures not only extraordinarily difficult but probably downright impossible.

A very different situation exists in Sweden. A highly homogeneous people (until the recent influx of immigrants, at any rate), Swedes have a long and settled tradition of consensus politics. Although the origins of the Swedish parliament go back some centuries, democratization arrived comparatively late. Not until 1917 was the power to choose the prime minister shifted from the king to the parliament. In that sense, Swedish democracy dates back to 1917. Proportional representation had already been introduced in parliamentary elections, however, at the beginning of the twentieth century. Yet neither proportional representation nor democratization diminished the long-standing Swedish tradition of consensus. As a Swedish political scientist has written:

> In the Swedish political tradition . . . "accountability" is seldom mentioned as a value. Instead, legitimacy is promoted by another strategy. By sharing power with the parties in opposition and including them in the rule of the country, the government is supposed to be regarded as representative for the people as a whole and consequently one that all can feel loyal to. To "reach consensus," to "find a common policy," to "capture the will of the people" have been the declared motives of Swedish politicians. *Representativeness* is the central norm of political culture.[14]

From an American perspective, the result can be unbelievable. In stark contrast to Holland and Switzerland, Swedish cabinets have frequently been drawn from a party or coalition that has actually *lacked* a majority of seats in parliament. In the past century, "minority governments have been by far the most common. The average parliamentary support enjoyed by governments between 1920 and 1994 has been 41.5 percent." You might well wonder how minority governments could ever get anything accomplished—or, for that matter, remain very long in office. The answer seems to be that in order to gain a broad consensus both in the parliament and in the country at large, even minority governments negotiate with representatives of parties *outside* the government. In short, even minority governments govern by consensus.

If you wonder why the Dutch, the Swiss, and the Swedes prefer proportionality to majoritarianism, the answer is fairly clear: not only does it seem to them much fairer but it also helps to achieve and maintain a broad consensus for government policies.

What is more, proportionality can strengthen consensus not just for policies but for democracy as well. The reason appears to be that proportionality results in fewer losers. To clarify this point let me overstate it: In a majoritarian system the only winners in elections are the citizens who happen to be in the majority; all the other citizens, being in the defeated minority, are losers. By contrast, in proportional systems with consensus governments, everyone—well, almost everyone—can win, not everything they hoped for perhaps but enough to leave them basically satisfied with their government.

Lest you suppose that these judgments are nothing more than interesting speculations, let me cite some persuasive supporting evidence.[15]

In a 1990 survey of citizens' views in eleven European democracies, respondents were asked how satisfied they were with "the way democracy works" in their country. They also reported how they voted in their country's last national election. Knowing the outcome of that election in each country, the authors of the study classified the respondents as winners or losers. The eleven countries were then arranged from the most majoritarian, Britain, to the most consensual, the Netherlands. The results, which the authors of the study describe as "robust," were pretty clear: In the more consensual countries, losers were almost as satisfied as the winners with the way democracy worked in their country. By contrast, in the more majoritarian countries, losers were much more likely to be dissatisfied.

To describe the results another way, suppose that in one country 70 percent of the winners but only 40 percent of the losers are satisfied with the working of democracy, a difference of 30 percent. In another country, say, 70 percent of the winners and 65 percent of the losers are satisfied, a difference of only 5 percent. In the study of eleven European democracies that I just mentioned, this difference in satisfaction with the way democracy worked decreased steadily from large differences in the most majoritarian countries like Britain—around 25 percent—to almost negligible differences in the most consensual countries like the Netherlands, where it was less than 5 percent.[16] Moreover, these results held up even when variations in such influences as economic performance, socioeconomic status, and political interest were taken into account.[17]

In short, if you live in a majoritarian country and your party comes in second or worse, you're likely to be dissatisfied with the way democracy works in your country. But if you live in a democratic country with a more consensual system and your party comes in second, or third, or maybe even fourth, you're likely to feel satisfied with the way democracy works because you know your views will still be represented in the government.

This is all fine, you might say, but can a consensus system produce effective governments—governments that can solve the problems that concern citizens? Might not majoritarian governments perform more effectively? In particular, hasn't our American constitutional system been just as effective as many consensus governments and perhaps even more effective than most in getting things done that citizens want? I'll turn to this question in a moment.

But before I do so, I want to call your attention to one salient aspect of our constitutional system: *The American constitutional system is not majoritarian*.

The American Hybrid

Whatever its hypothetical advantages might be, the majoritarian vision is not applicable to the American system of government. Although our system is not proportional, neither is it majoritarian. Whether by rational intention or by an understandable inability to foresee the consequences, or both, James Madison and his fellow delegates created a constitutional system that is a hybrid of proportionality and majoritarianism.

Three majorities. It is true that two parties dominate our political landscape more completely than in any other established democracy. Yet even when one party wins not only the presidency but also majorities in both the Senate and House, three different popular majorities are at work; the composition of each of the three majorities does not match the others; and their representatives do not necessarily agree. I would not say that this feature is necessarily undesirable, but undesirable consequences do show up when it is combined with other aspects of our system.

Divided government. To begin with, one party may fail to win control of all three branches. Indeed, during the past half-century, control of the presidency and both houses of Congress by a single party has become a rarity. As David Mayhew comments in *Divided We Govern,* "Since World War II, divided party control of the American national government has come to seem normal."[18] From 1946 to 2000, the three branches have been divided between the two parties more than six years out of every ten. Our constitution not only permits divided government, it cannot prevent divided government. And it provides no way out except by elections at fixed intervals—elections that may only reproduce the existing divisions or inaugurate new ones.

Does divided government matter? In particular, do periods of divided government make it more difficult for the three branches to agree on national policies requiring legislation—in short, do these periods make a stalemate easier? The evidence is mixed. In a landmark study of the period between the elections of 1946 and 1990, David Mayhew found no "relation worth crediting between the incidence of important laws and whether party control was unified or divided."[19] A subsequent analysis of the period from 1947 to 1994, however, concluded that important legislation is more likely to be passed in periods of unified government. The difference between divided and unified government is particularly marked when all three branches are under the unified control of the more activist of the two parties, the Democrats.[20]

The president: consensual, majoritarian, neither, both? At the apex of this complex structure of political institutions sits—or stands, as the case may be—the American presidency, an office with no equivalent in any of the other established democracies or, so far as I am aware, in any other democratic country.

It is difficult, indeed impossible, to fit the presidency into the simple categories of consensual or majoritarian. One obstacle to straightforward classification is the president's combination of roles. Most notably, whereas in the other older democracies the roles of prime minister and ceremonial head of state are separated, in our system they are blended, not only constitutionally but also in popular expectations. We expect our president to serve both as chief executive and as a sort of ceremonial, dignified, American-style elected monarch and moral exemplar.

The mix of roles was present from the beginning. Although during the early years the vituperation of presidents in the press often far exceeded boundaries now regarded as acceptable, in order to maintain the dignity of the office presidents rarely addressed the general public, except possibly on official occasions; and when they did they rarely employed popular rhetoric or discussed their own policies. In these respects, if no others, they acted less like politicians than monarchs or ceremonial heads of state. Indeed, until the 1830s, presidential candidates did not make campaign speeches at all; and until Woodrow Wilson broke a century-old taboo in 1912, no president had ever "stumped on his own behalf."[21]

Beginning with Andrew Jackson, however, presidents had already begun to make the audacious claim that by virtue of their election, they alone represented the *entire* people, or at least a majority. Some would even assert that their election endowed them with a "mandate" for their policies. To the extent that the claim of a mandate was accepted, it would increase the acceptability of a president's policies by clothing them with the legitimacy of popular sovereignty.

Despite the frequency with which newly elected presidents stake a claim to a mandate, the closer you inspect the chain of assumptions that are supposed to support the claim, the more fragile the links appear.[22] It requires an extraordinary leap of faith to infer the views of voters from nothing more than the way they cast their votes for president. Although systematic opinion surveys provide a much firmer basis for understanding public attitudes and expectations, the claim to a presidential mandate based on nothing more than the outcome of an election antedated systematic surveys by more than a century. And even since the beginning of systematic opinion surveys in the 1940s, presidents and their followers (and pundits) have typically based their shaky claim to a mandate on nothing more than the election returns, which could not possibly reveal whether presidential policies accorded with voters' preferences. Since the 1940s that concordance is more likely to come from scrupulous attention to public opinion surveys than from reading the tea leaves of the election results.

Presidential claims to represent "the American people" together with efforts to promote particular national policies are elements in the general mixture of roles that distinguishes the American presidency and makes it neither simply majoritarian nor simply consensual.

This mix of roles seems to be generally accepted by Americans. We want our presidents, it seems, to be simultaneously shrewd politicians and gifted statesmen. We expect them to live in both the real world of daily politics and an imaginary world above politics. Most of us understand that to succeed in office a president must be an active and forceful partisan, a party leader, and the negotiator and deal-maker who massages, cajoles, bribes, threatens, and coerces Congress to secure both votes and support if promises and policies are to be realized.

But we also expect our president to serve as a moral example for us all, to stand as an icon on which we can devoutly project qualities of intelligence, knowledge, understanding, compassion, and character far above those we expect in ordinary beings like ourselves. Because no mortal can meet these exalted standards, we have often savaged a president while he is in office and then exalted him in memory. In office, we may portray a president as a cartoonish bungler. But after departing the White House, or this world, we ignore the warts and scars and paint an idealized portrait of a noble and exemplary figure.

Ambivalence toward the presidency is deeply ingrained in our American culture. As children we learn to worship our presidents for their greatness;[23] as adults we deride them for failing to achieve the greatness of their mythic predecessors. In choosing among candidates for the presidency we yearn for perfection; yet our only realistic choices are among flawed human beings who live with all the moral ambiguities required by the life of politics. In short, the impossible mix of roles an American president is expected to play places a heavy burden not only on the incumbent, but more important, on American voters.

Accountability. Holding the government accountable for its actions may be an even greater burden for voters. Where are we to place responsibility for the conduct of our government? When we go to the polls, whom can we hold accountable for the successes and failures of national policies? The president? The House? The Senate? The unelected Supreme Court? Or, given our federal system, the states, where governments are, in their complexity, a microcosm of the national government?

Even for those who spend their lives studying politics, these can be extremely difficult questions to answer. I, for one, am inclined to think that compared with the political systems of the other advanced democratic countries, ours is among the most opaque, complex, confusing, and difficult to understand.

We see, then, that our hybrid system, which is neither majoritarian nor proportional, may possess the advantages of neither and the defects of both. If it fails to ensure the fairness promised by the proportional vision, it also fails to provide the clear accountability promised by the majoritarian vision.

Democratic Effectiveness

To all this you might say: Even if the American hybrid may have some shortcomings when it is viewed in a comparative perspective, isn't it just as effective as other governments in dealing with the issues that concern American citizens?

Once again, we cannot answer this question responsibly without facing up to some severe methodological problems. Our twenty-two democratic countries differ in so many ways that teasing out the effects that we can reasonably attribute to constitutional systems is a pretty formidable task. Take *size*. The population of the United States is sixty times larger than Norway's, fifty times Denmark's, thirty-seven times Switzerland's, thirty times Sweden's, and nearly a thousand times larger than Iceland's, which is somewhat smaller in population than Tampa, Florida.

Although the effects of population size on democratic political life are extremely difficult to measure, they can hardly be ignored.[24]

Or consider *diversity:* in a very general way, diversity tends to increase with size.[25] Yet can we truly say that the United States is more diverse than Switzerland, or than our neighbor Canada?

Add in one more variable: *relative affluence*. Although Norway and Costa Rica are both relatively small in population—there are around 4.5 million Norwegians and around 3.7 million Costa Ricans—Norway's GNP per capita is fourteen times that of Costa Rica.[26]

How much do these differences in size, diversity, and relative affluence affect political life and public policy? Despite the difficulties presented by national variations like these, comparative data can help us gain some appreciation of the way in which American performance compares with that of other advanced democratic countries.[27] When the United States is ranked with other established democracies on such matters as the rate of incarceration, the ratio of poor to rich, economic growth, social expenditures, energy efficiency, foreign aid and the like, its performance is something less than impressive. (See Appendix B, Table 5.) Two areas in which our country ranks highest are hardly achievements of which we can be proud. On the percentage of the population we incarcerate, we come out a clear winner, while our ratio of rich to poor is higher than that of most other countries. We rank in the bottom third—and on some measures close to the bottom of the bottom third—on voter turnout, state welfare measures, energy efficiency, and the representation of women in the national legislature. What is more, in spite of our good showing on economic growth, we are almost dead last in our social expenditures. Finally, even though many Americans believe that we are too generous in our economic aid to other countries, among nineteen democratic countries we are at the very bottom.

In his comparison of consensual and majoritarian systems in thirty-six countries, Arend Lijphart concluded that "majoritarian democracies do not outperform the consensus democracies on macroeconomic management and the control of violence—in fact, the consensus democracies have the slightly better record—but the consensus democracies do clearly outperform the majoritarian democracies with regard to the quality of democracy and democratic representation as well as with regard to what I have called the kindness and gentleness of their public policy orientations."[28]

Paraphrasing Lijphart's conclusion, I find no convincing evidence that our hybrid outperforms systems that are either more fully consensual systems or more fully majoritarian. On the contrary, compared with other democratic countries our performance appears, on balance, to be mediocre at best.

How much does our performance have to do with our constitutional system? To tease out the extent of that connection would be extraordinarily difficult, perhaps impossible, and I am going to leave that task to others.[29]

It seems reasonably clear, however, that a constitutional system better designed to achieve such democratic goals as the protection of fundamental rights, fair representation, and greater consensus does not necessarily come at the price of governmental effectiveness, much less the stability of the democratic system itself.

If this is so, then do we not have every reason to undertake a serious and responsible examination of pos-

sible alternatives to our present American Constitution?
Or, at the very least, isn't it time—well-past time—that
we stop thinking of our Constitution as a sacred text
and begin to think of it as nothing more, or less, than a
means for achieving democratic goals?

CHAPTER 6

Why Not a More Democratic Constitution?

I BEGAN BY POSING THIS QUESTION: WHY SHOULD WE Americans uphold our Constitution? Let me now change the question slightly: What kind of constitution *should* we feel obliged to uphold?

I mean, of course, an American constitution—not necessarily our present Constitution, but a constitution that, after careful and prolonged deliberation, we and our fellow citizens conclude is best designed to serve our fundamental political ends, goals, and values.

The Constitution as National Icon

I am well aware that in expressing reservations about the Constitution, as I have in these essays, I may be judged guilty of casting stones at a national icon. "From the time of the founding fathers," a historian has recently remarked, "there [has] been a sacred aura about the Constitution, manifest in holiday political rhetoric." During the years between the two World Wars, worship of the Constitution "acquired the trappings of a religious cult."[1] This reverential attitude continues. In a telephone survey of one thousand adult U.S. citizens in 1997, 71 percent said they strongly agreed with the statement that they were proud of the Constitution; another 20 percent somewhat agreed.[2] In a 1999 survey, 85 percent said they thought the Constitution is a major reason why "America has been successful during this past century."[3]

I don't dismiss the importance of icons for strengthening beliefs, religious or political, nor do I dismiss the utility of myth and ritual in helping to foster national cohesion. But a faith that rests on little more than a general conformity to conventional beliefs is a fragile foundation for nationhood—not to say for democracy. I want therefore to suggest an alternative.

The only legitimate constitution for a democratic people, it seems to me, is one crafted to serve democratic ends. Viewed from this perspective an American constitution ought to be the best that we can design for enabling politically equal citizens to govern themselves under laws and government policies that have been adopted and are maintained with their rational consent.

This is hardly a novel view. What I am suggesting is that a constitution derives its legitimacy from a moral and political judgment announced to the world more than two centuries ago. This judgment (slightly modified from the original) asserts:

> That all *human beings* are created equal, that they are endowed by their Creator with certain inalienable Rights, that among these are Life, Liberty, and the Pursuit of Happiness. That to secure these rights, Governments are instituted among *a people,* deriving their just powers from the consent of the governed. That whenever a Form of government becomes destructive of these ends, it is the Right of the people to alter or abolish it, and to institute new government, laying its foundation on such principles and organizing its powers in such a form, as to them shall seem most likely to effect their Safety and Happiness.

But two questions immediately arise. First, is political equality a realistic goal? Second, is it really a desirable goal?[4]

Is Political Equality a Realistic Goal?

Some of you may dismiss the noble words I have just quoted as obviously false. If anything about equality is self-evident, you might object, it is that human beings *aren't* equal. Whether by genes, birth, luck, achievements, or whatever, we aren't equal in education, cultural endowments, social and communication skills, intelligence, motor skills, incomes, wealth, the country in which we live, and so on. Though this objection is a commonplace, it wholly misses the point. The men who wrote and adopted the American Declaration of Independence hardly needed to be reminded of such elementary matters. They knew too much about the ways of the world to make assertions that were obviously contradicted by everyday human experience. But, of course, they didn't mean the Declaration to be understood as a statement of fact. They meant it to be understood as a *moral* statement. Human equality, they were insisting, is a moral and even a religious standard against which it is right and proper to judge a political system.

Yet ideal standards might rise so far beyond human reach as to be irrelevant. Is political equality so remote from human possibilities that we might just as well forget it?

I need hardly remind you of the enormous and persistent barriers to political equality and, indeed, to human equality in general.[5] Consider that elemental and age-old barrier arising from differences in the treatment of men and women. The authors of the familiar words about equality that I just quoted and the fifty-five delegates to the Second Continental Congress who voted to adopt the Declaration in July 1776, were, of course, all men, none of whom had the slightest intention of extending the suffrage or many other basic political and civil rights to women—who by the laws of that time and for a full century after were the legal property of their fathers or husbands.

Nor did the worthy supporters of the Declaration mean to include slaves or, for that matter, free persons of African origin, who were a substantial fraction of the population in almost all the colonies that claimed the right to become independent self-governing republics. The principal author of the Declaration, Thomas Jefferson, owned several hundred slaves, none of whom he freed during his life.[6] It was not until more than four score and seven years later (to borrow a poetic phrase from Lincoln's Gettysburg Address) that slavery was legally abolished in the United States by force of arms and constitutional enactment. And it took yet another century before the rights of African Americans to participate in political life began to be effectively enforced in the American South. Now, two generations later, Americans white and black still bear the deep wounds that slavery and its aftermath inflicted on human equality, freedom, dignity, and respect.

Nor did our noble Declaration mean to include the people who for thousands of years had inhabited the lands that Europeans colonized and came to occupy. We are all familiar with the story of how the settlers denied homes, land, place, freedom, dignity, and humanity to these earlier peoples of America, whose descendants even today continue to suffer from the effects of their treatment throughout several centuries, when their most elementary claims to legal, economic, and political—not to say social—standing as equal human beings were rejected, often by violence; more recently, this lengthy period has been followed by neglect and indifference.

All this in a country that visitors from Europe, such

as Alexis de Tocqueville, portrayed (correctly, I think) as displaying a passion for equality stronger than they had ever observed elsewhere.

Yet, despite the fact that throughout human history equality has often been denied in practice, throughout the past several centuries many claims to equality, including political equality, have come to be much more strongly reinforced by institutions, practices, and behavior. Although this monumental historical movement toward equality is in some respects worldwide, it has been most conspicuous in such democratic countries as Britain, France, the United States, the Scandinavian countries, the Netherlands, and others.

In the opening pages of the first volume of *Democracy in America*, Tocqueville pointed to the inexorable increase in the equality of conditions among his French countrymen "at intervals of fifty years, beginning with the eleventh century." Nor was this revolution taking place in only his own country: "Whithersoever we turn our eyes," he wrote, "we shall witness the same continual revolution throughout the whole of Christendom." He goes on to say, "The gradual development of the equality of conditions is . . . a providential fact, and it possesses all the characteristics of a Divine decree: it is universal, it is durable, it constantly eludes all human interference, and all events as well as men contribute to its progress."[7]

We may wish to grant Tocqueville a certain measure of hyperbole in this passage. We may also want to note that in the second volume that he published several years later, he was more troubled by what he viewed as some of the undesirable consequences of democracy and equality. I shall return to his concerns in a moment. Even so, he did not doubt that a continuing advance of democracy and equality was inevitable. And if we look back today to the changes since his time, like Tocqueville in his own day we may well be amazed at the extent to which ideas and practices that respect and promote political equality have advanced across so much of the world—as, for that matter, have some aspects of a broader human equality as well.

As to political equality, consider the incredible spread of democratic ideas, institutions, and practices during the century that just ended. In 1900, 48 countries were fully or moderately independent countries. Of these, only 8 possessed all the other basic institutions of representative democracy, and in only 1 of these, New Zealand, had women gained the right to vote. Furthermore, these 8 countries contained no more than 10–12 percent of the world's population. At the opening of our present century, among some 190 countries the political institutions and practices of modern representative democracy, including universal suffrage, exist in around 85, at levels comparable to those in Britain, western Europe, and the United States. These countries include almost 5 out of every 10 inhabitants of the globe today.[8]

In Britain, the working classes and women *were* enfranchised, and more. Men and women of middle, lower-middle, and working-class origins gained access not only to the House of Commons and its facilities but to the cabinet and even the post of prime minister. And the hereditary peers in the House of Lords have, after all, at last been sent packing—well, most of them anyway. In the United States, too, women were enfranchised. The Voting Rights Act of 1965, which protected the right of African Americans to vote, did in fact become law; the law was actually enforced; and African Americans have become a significant force in American political life. I wish I could say that the miserable condition of so many Native Americans had greatly changed for the better, but that sad legacy of human injustice remains with us.

Although we must admit to persistent failures and continuing obstacles, if we assume that beliefs about equality are hopelessly anemic contestants in the struggle against the powerful forces that generate inequalities, we cannot account for the enormous gains in human equality achieved over the past two centuries.

How Does Greater Political Equality Come About?

In the face of so many obstacles, how does greater equality—or better, a reduction in some inequalities—ever come about? Although no brief summary can do justice to an explanation of the historical variations and complexities in the process by which changes toward equality take place—and here I have in mind mainly political equality—a summary of the most important elements would probably run something like this:

Despite fervent efforts by privileged elites to promote views intended to give legitimacy to their superior power and status, together with their own unquestioning belief in the rightness of their entitlements (think of the Federalists!), many members of subordinate groups doubt that the inferior position assigned to them by their self-proclaimed superiors is really justified. James Scott has shown pretty convincingly that people who have been relegated to subordinate status by history, structure, and elite belief systems are much less likely to be taken in by the dominant ideology than members of the upper strata are prone to assume.[9] Given the open or concealed rejection of the elite ideology by members of the subordinate groups, a change in conditions, whether in ideas, beliefs, generations, structures, resources, or whatever, begins to offer the subordinate groups new opportunities to express their grievances. And given these new opportunities and moved by anger, resentment, a sense of injustice, a prospect of greater individual or group opportunities, group loyalty, or other motives, some members of the subordinate groups begin to press for change by whatever means are available. Some members of the dominant group begin to support the claims of the subordinate strata. Privileged insiders ally themselves with outsiders. Insiders may do so for a variety of reasons: moral convictions, compassion, opportunism, fear of the consequences of disorder, dangers to property and the legitimacy of the regime arising from widening discontent, and even the real or imagined possibility of revolution.[10]

So a seismic shift occurs: extension of the franchise, legal protection of basic rights, political competition from leaders of hitherto subordinate groups, election to public office, changes in law and policy, and so on. In the United States, Civil Rights Acts were passed in 1957, 1960, and most crucial of all, 1965. What is more, they were enforced. African Americans began to seize their opportunities to vote—and among other things soon tossed out the police officials who had violently enforced their subordination. In India, the scheduled castes have begun to vote in substantial numbers for leaders and parties who are drawn from their own strata and committed to reducing discrimination against them. Though changes toward equality may be and typically are incremental, a series of incremental changes can, in time, mount to a revolution.

By such processes, then, a certain measure of political equality and democracy have been obtained in some countries despite enormous and persistent obstacles to human equality.

Is Political Equality a Justifiable Goal?

Yet even if a greater degree of political equality and democracy can be achieved, are these goals really *de-*

sirable? What's more, are they so desirable that we should make the constitution of a democratic country—in particular that of the United States—subordinate to achieving these ends?

The desirability of political equality and thus of democracy follows, in my view, from two fundamental judgments. One is moral, the other practical.

The moral judgment holds that all human beings are of equal intrinsic worth; that no person is intrinsically superior in worth to another; and that the good or interests of each person ought to be given equal consideration.[11] Let me call this the *assumption of intrinsic equality*.

Yet if we accept this moral judgment, a deeply troublesome question immediately arises: Who or what group is the best qualified to decide what the good or interests of a person really are? Clearly the answer will vary, depending on the situation, the kinds of decisions, and the persons involved. But if we restrict our focus to the government of a state, then it seems to me that the safest and most prudent assumption would run something like this: Among adults, none are so better qualified than others to govern that they should be entrusted with complete and final authority over the government of the state.[12]

Although we might reasonably add refinements and qualifications to this prudential judgment, it is difficult for me to see how a significantly different proposition could be defended, particularly if we draw on crucial historical cases in which substantial numbers of persons were denied equal citizenship. Does anyone today really believe that when the working classes, women, and racial and ethnic minorities were excluded from political participation, their interests were adequately considered and protected by those who were privileged to govern over them?

Does Political Equality Threaten Liberty?

Like many desirable goals, political equality might conflict with—and may indeed do harm to—other important goals, ends, values. If so, shouldn't our pursuit of political equality be tempered by our justifiable desire to attain these other goals?

It is frequently said that equality conflicts with liberty and fundamental rights. Like many others, Tocqueville appears to have believed so.

But before I turn to his remarks, I cannot forgo adding that I am amazed by a frequent assertion about the supposed conflict between liberty and equality that makes no mention of what would seem to me to be an absolutely essential requirement of any reasonable discussion about the relation between the two. Whenever we talk about liberty, freedom, or rights, are we not obliged to answer the question: Liberty or rights for whom? When we speak of freedom, liberty, or rights it seems to me essential that we go beyond answering the question, "What liberty or right?" An answer to that question only specifies the *domain* of liberty. But we are also obliged to answer the question, "Liberty *for whom?*"[13]

Keeping this question in mind, let me return to Tocqueville. His view, if I understand him correctly, was roughly this: An equality of condition among a people helps to make democracy possible, perhaps even inevitable. But the very equality of condition that makes democracy possible also carries dangers to liberty. Let me paraphrase Tocqueville:

> Since the very essence of democratic government is the absolute sovereignty of the majority, which nothing in democratic states is capable of resisting, a majority necessarily has the power to oppress a minority. Just as a man with absolute power may misuse it, so may a majority. Given an equality of condition among citizens, we may expect that in democratic countries a wholly new species of oppression will arise. Among citizens all equal and alike, the supreme power, the democratic government, acting in response to the will of the majority, will create a society with a network of small complicated rules, minute and uniform, that none can escape. Ultimately, then, the citizens of a democratic country will be reduced to nothing better than a flock of timid and industrious animals, of which the government is the shepherd.[14]

If I have fairly summarized Tocqueville, how should we interpret his forecast in the light of subsequent developments? After all, we have the advantage, as he did not, of two centuries of experience with modern democratic institutions. Some readers have interpreted these passages in Tocqueville as foreshadowing mass society, while to others Tocqueville expected that mass democracy would be the seed of twentieth-century authoritarian and totalitarian systems. Yet, if we read the passages as a forecast of the way in which democratic countries would tend to evolve, I think we are bound to conclude that Tocqueville was just dead wrong. When we examine the course of democratic development over the past two centuries, and particularly over the century just ended, what we find is a pattern of democratic development that stands in total contradiction to such a prediction. We find instead that as democratic institutions become more deeply rooted in a country, so do fundamental political rights, liberties, and opportunities. As a democratic government matures in a country, the likelihood that it will give way to an authoritarian regime approaches zero. Democracy can, as we all know, collapse into dictatorship. But breakdowns are extraordinarily rare in mature democracies; they occur instead in countries that encounter times of great crisis and stress when their democratic institutions are relatively new. Crisis appears to be inevitable in the life of every country. Even mature democratic countries have had to face wars, economic depression, large-scale unemployment, terrorism, and other challenges. But they did not collapse into authoritarian regimes.

In the twentieth century, on something like seventy occasions democracies have given way to nondemocratic regimes. Yet with very few exceptions, these breakdowns have occurred in countries where democratic institutions were very new—less than a generation old. Indeed, the only clear-cut case of a democratic breakdown in a country where democratic institutions had existed for twenty years or more seems to be Uruguay in 1973. In the same year, Chile provided a less clear-cut case because of restrictions on the suffrage that had only recently been lifted. The Weimar Republic had existed fewer than fourteen years before the Nazi takeover. In all three countries the path to collapse bore no relation to the Tocquevillean scenario.

Nor, as we know, is that scenario confirmed by the older or mature democracies. As I indicated in the previous chapter, we can find some small variations among these countries in their protection of basic rights. But they all maintain these rights well above the threshold necessary for democracy. Have the fundamental rights and liberties of citizens grown steadily narrower or less secure over the past half-century? I do not see how an affirmative answer to this question could be seriously maintained. Much as I admire Tocqueville, on this issue, he, like the Framers, could not foresee the future of democratic government.

Far from being a threat to fundamental rights and liberties, political equality requires them as anchors for democratic institutions. To see why this is so, let me once again view democracy as, ideally at least, a political system designed for citizens of a state who are willing to treat one another, for political purposes, as *political* equals. Citizens might view one another as unequal in other respects. Indeed, they almost certainly would. But if they were to assume that all citizens possess equal rights to participate, directly or indirectly through their elected representatives, in making the policies, rules, laws, or other decisions that citizens are expected (or required) to obey, then the government of their state would, ideally, have to satisfy several criteria.

Let me list them here without amplification. To be fully democratic, a state would have to provide: *rights, liberties, and opportunities* for effective participation; voting equality; the ability to acquire sufficient understanding of policies and their consequences; and the means by which the citizen body could maintain adequate control of the agenda of government policies and decisions. Finally, as we now understand the ideal, in order to be *fully* democratic, a state would have to ensure that all, or at any rate most, permanent adult residents under its jurisdiction would possess the rights of citizenship.

As we know, the democratic ideal that I have just described is too demanding to be achieved in the actual world of human society. To accomplish it as far as may be possible under the imperfect conditions of the real world, certain political institutions for governing the state would be required. Moreover, since the eighteenth century these institutions have had to be suitable for governing a state encompassing a large territory, such as a country.

There is no need to describe here the basic political institutions of a modern democratic country; but it should be obvious that just as in the ideal, so too in actual practice, democratic government presupposes that its citizens possess a body of fundamental *rights, liberties, and opportunities*. These include the rights to vote in the election of officials in free and fair elections; to run for elective office; to free expression; to form and participate in independent political organizations; to have access to independent sources of information; and to have rights to other freedoms and opportunities that may be necessary for the effective operation of the political institutions of large-scale democracy.

Both as an ideal and as an actual set of political institutions, democracy is necessarily, then, a system of rights, liberties, and opportunities. These are required not merely by definition. They are required in order for a democratic system of government to exist in the real world. If we consider these political rights, liberties, and opportunities as in some sense fundamental, then in theory and in practice, democracy does not conflict with liberty. On the contrary, democratic institutions are necessary for the existence of some of our most fundamental rights and opportunities. If these political institutions, including the rights, liberties, and opportunities they embody, do not exist in a country, then to that extent the country is not democratic. When they disappear, as they did in Weimar Germany, Uruguay, and Chile, then democracy disappears; and when democracy disappears, as it did in these countries, then so do these fundamental right, liberties, and opportunities. Likewise, when democracy reappeared in these countries so, necessarily, did these fundamental rights, liberties, and opportunities. The connection, then, is not in any sense accidental. It is inherent.

The links between political equality and democracy, on the one hand, and fundamental rights, liberties, and opportunities, on the other, run even deeper. If a country is to maintain its democratic institutions through its inevitable crises, it will need a body of norms, beliefs, and habits that provide support for the institutions in good times and bad—a democratic culture transmitted from one generation to the next. But a democratic culture is unlikely to be sharply bounded. A democratic culture will support not only the fundamental rights, liberties, and opportunities that democratic institutions require. People who share a democratic culture will, I think inevitably, also endorse and support an even greater sphere of rights, liberties, and opportunities. Surely the history of recent centuries demonstrates that it is precisely in democratic countries that liberties thrive.

★   ★   ★

IF WE BELIEVE THAT ALL HUMAN BEINGS ARE CREATED equal, that they are endowed with certain inalienable rights, that among these are life, liberty, and the pursuit of happiness, that to secure these rights governments are instituted among a people, deriving their just powers from the consent of the governed, then we are obliged to support the goal of political equality.

Political equality requires democratic political institutions.

The supposed conflict between liberty and political equality is spurious, first, because an inherent part of democratic political institutions is a substantial body of fundamental rights, liberties, and opportunities; and, second, because a people committed to democracy and its political institutions will almost certainly expand the sphere of fundamental rights, liberties, and opportunities well beyond those strictly necessary for democracy and political equality.

Among a people committed to democracy and political equality, a constitution should serve those ends by helping to maintain political institutions that foster political equality among citizens and all the necessary rights, liberties, and opportunities that are essential to the existence of political equality and a democratic government.

CHAPTER 7

Some Reflections on the Prospects for a More Democratic Constitution

———————◆———————

I N A 1987 SURVEY THAT REVEALED STRONG SUPPORT among Americans for the Constitution on the whole, the results of one question stand out. When respondents were asked, "How good a job has [the system of government established by the Constitution] done in treating all people equally?" Fifty-one percent answered that it had done a bad job, 8 percent expressed no opinion, and a minority of 41 percent said that it had done a good job.[1]

If we want to enjoy a system of government that performs better in treating all people equally—at least in their roles as democratic citizens—what might we do? As I said at the beginning of Chapter 1, my aim in these essays is not to offer a set of specific proposals for changes in the Constitution but rather to encourage a change in the way we *think* about our Constitution. How then might we begin to think realistically about changing it? What possibilities would actually be open to a body of framers in the early years of the twenty-first century? What limits on the range of possibilities should they expect to confront?

The Limited Role of a Constitution

To begin with, tomorrow's constitutional reformers would be wise to recognize that no matter what a constitution prescribes on paper, it can achieve only a limited range of goals. For example, as I pointed out in Chapter 5, no constitution can ensure democracy in a country where the conditions favorable to democracy are absent. To preserve and improve these favorable conditions would accomplish far more in achieving a more democratic order than any changes in the constitution.

The Framers of 1787 were well aware of their limits. One of the striking features of the constitution they wrote is its admirable brevity. Depending on the style in which it is printed, the written text runs fifteen to twenty pages, plus another five to seven pages of amendments. What enables the written Constitution to achieve this brevity is its almost exclusive focus on just three matters: *structures, powers,* and *rights*.

Most of the Constitution is devoted to the first two matters, structures and the powers allocated to these structures. Provisions about the third matter, rights, are found mainly in the Bill of Rights and in later amendments. An important feature of these constitutional rights is that they are guaranteed almost entirely by imposing constitutional *limits* on the government. The Constitution tacitly assumes that citizens themselves will somehow possess the opportunities and resources necessary in order for them to act on their rights. I'll come back to this assumption in a moment.

Constitutional Structures

Let me say a few words about structures. I am inclined to believe that three, and possibly four, structural elements in our constitutional system are not, realistically speaking, open to change in the foreseeable future.

Federalism. One element is our federal system. Just as the Framers knew that they could not abolish the states, constitutional reformers today should probably assume that the states will remain—and in my judgment they should remain—as fundamental units in a federal government that are endowed with significant powers. As has been true for two centuries, the question of how power is shared between the federal government and the states will persist as a subject of endless dispute. But I do not believe that constitutional framers today would or should attempt to dissolve the existing states.

Presidentialism. A second limit on constitutional reform, I believe, is our presidential system. We may be able to alter it a bit around the edges with amendments or changed practices, but the option of a parliamentary system is, I would guess, simply not attractive to most Americans. We have so deeply invested ourselves in the mythical aspects of the presidency that short of some constitutional breakdown, which I neither foresee nor, certainly, wish for, we won't seriously consider changing it. For better or worse, we Americans are stuck with a presidential system.

Inequality in representation.   The other feature that I fear constitutional reformers would be unable change is the gross inequality in representation resulting from the fixed allocation of two senators to each state without regard to population. Let me remind you again that Section 3 of Article I reads: "The Senate of the United States shall be composed of two Senators from each State for six Years, and each Senator shall have one Vote." A constitutional amendment to change this provision faces two formidable obstacles. The first makes it most unlikely that any constitutional amendment to change the composition of the Senate will be adopted. The second makes it virtually impossible. First, under Article V of the Constitution, you may recall, amendments can be proposed only with a *two-thirds* vote in both houses or by a convention supported by *two-thirds* of the state legislatures; and they can be adopted only after ratification by the legislatures or conventions in *three-fourths* of the states. I can't help thinking that at least thirteen of the least populated states would exercise their veto to prevent the adoption of any amendment that would reduce their influence in the Senate. But in the highly improbable event that such an amendment might somehow make its way past this formidable obstacle, the second barrier promises to be totally impregnable. "No State, without its Consent," Article V of the Constitution concludes, "shall be deprived of its equal Suffrage in the Senate."

In effect, those fifteen words end all possibility of amending the constitution in order to reduce the unequal representation of citizens in the Senate. So we are destined, it seems, to be saddled indefinitely with a greater degree of unequal representation in the upper house than exists in any of the other established democracies.

If I am correct about these three fixed elements— federalism, presidentialism, and unequal representation in the Senate—they in turn seem likely to impose other limits on what today's framers might accomplish.

The electoral college. For example, what can we do about changing the electoral college? In Chapter 4 I showed how the inequality of representation in the Senate reproduces itself, though somewhat weakened, in the electoral college. It plays out yet again in diminishing the chances that the Constitution can be amended to replace the electoral college with a system of popular election. Consequently, I suggested, the relative desirability of three possible solutions to the problem of unequal representation in the electoral college is inversely related to the probability of their enactment.

Consensual, majoritarian, or neither? I have already expressed some sympathy toward a consensual system as an alternative to a majoritarian system. The United States, I suggested, is neither one nor the other. It is a hybrid that just might have the vices of both and the virtues of neither.

That our political leaders manage much of the time to avoid complete deadlock and make the system work—more or less—is testimony, I think, to their exceptional political skills, which tend to be vastly undervalued in the media and among ordinary citizens. I have also suggested that the necessary wheeling and dealing, the inevitable behind-the-scenes compromises, and the unavoidable gap between public rhetoric and the mutual concessions among insiders, result in a political system so opaque and so at odds with general conceptions of public virtue that it weakens both civic understanding and citizens' confidence in our political institutions.

If we are unlikely to change either our presidential system or our severely unequal representation in the Senate, then it will also be very difficult to bring about some constitutional options that otherwise could be, and should be, seriously considered. In particular, I am not entirely sure that we can redesign our present hybrid so that it facilitates either greater consensus or stronger majoritarianism.

Neither alternative can exist without an appropriate political culture. Yet, a system designed to be consensual would harbor a serious danger if it were not strongly implanted in a political culture that fosters agreement. Lacking the appropriate political culture, a constitutional design intended for a consensual system would enable a minority to veto any changes from the status quo that threaten its privileges, as the Southern states did before the Civil War. Or a regionally privileged minority could extort concessions from the majority by threatening to use its veto, as the Southern states did when they compelled the rest of the country to abandon efforts to protect the civil rights of African-Americans after the Civil War.

I am inclined to believe that our political culture—unlike, say, that of Sweden, Switzerland, or Holland—would prevent a consensual design from realizing its potential advantages.

The corresponding fear about a strictly majoritarian system is that it might fail to provide the leaders of a majority with adequate incentives to seek greater consensus before they invoke their power as a majority. I'm not raising again here the issue of liberty versus political equality that I discussed earlier. Even if the leaders of a majority were to maintain the fullest respect for the democratic rights of minorities, they might see slight reason to explore options that would achieve a wider range of agreement and support than they need to push through a law or policy by majority vote.

The ideal solution, it seems to me, would be a political system that provides strong incentives for political leaders to search for the broadest feasible agreement before adopting a law or policy and yet allows the decision to be made, if need be, by majority vote—always, of course, within the limits set by the need to preserve fundamental democratic rights. No majority should have the right, moral or constitutional, to foreclose decisions by future majorities.

Here again, I fear that this ideal solution may not be open to us so long as severely unequal representation in the Senate allows some geographical minorities to block decisions by representatives elected by a majority of their fellow citizens. Because of this minority veto, the search for consensus could easily turn into what might be harshly described as extortion and blackmail by a minority of Senators.

Although this barrier to majority rule may be impossible to change, rules of the Senate that further compound the power of privileged minorities might be more amenable to change, as, in my view, they definitely should be. For example, it is doubtful that our futile and counterproductive policy toward Cuba would have remained so long in effect were it not for the ability of a handful of U.S. Senators to extort from Congress and the president the policies they favor, in return for their support on other issues.

So we arrive at this unhappy conclusion: The Framers of 1787 appear to have limited today's framers to a system that is neither consensual nor majoritarian but is a hybrid that possesses the vices of both and the virtues of neither.

Hidden costs and uncertainties.   The difficulty of transforming a long-established political culture into one appropriate to a new and different constitutional structure—one more consensual, say, or more majoritarian—illustrates yet another problem. Major constitutional change involves large hidden costs and a great uncertainty. The hidden costs arise because of the need to abandon familiar habits, practices, beliefs, and understandings that exist among the political elites and that are embedded in the popular culture as well. Creating an appropriate political culture may be almost as far beyond the capacities of constitutional framers today as it was for the Framers in 1787. What is more, even if our knowledge about the likely consequences of alternative constitutional structures is immeasurably better than that of the Framers, after two centuries of experience with different democratic constitutions predicting the outcome of major changes remains fraught with considerable uncertainty.

Powers

Are the constitutional powers of the states, the federal government, and the three main branches of the federal government appropriate to our democratic needs and values today? An attempt to answer this daunting question would so far exceed my limits here that I shall simply call attention to its relevance and importance.

Rights

As with powers, the subject of rights is so vast that I can do no more than sketch a view that seems to me useful for appraising fundamental rights in the context of a democratic country's constitution.

It is a standard view in jurisprudence that rights imply duties: in order for a right to be effectively exercised, government officials and others must assume the duty of protecting the right against persons who seek to violate it. A less-common assumption, but one present by implication, is that rights also imply opportunities: your *right* to vote is meaningless if you don't actually have an *opportunity* to vote. So too with freedom of expression. What would a right to free speech mean to you if you didn't have any opportunity to speak freely?

Now I want to add a fourth element to our discussion. To rights, duties, and opportunities I would add *resources*.[2] Suppose, for example, that voting booths were placed by officials in locations far from the homes of many citizens and were open for only one hour in mid-morning: most citizens would lack both opportunities and resources necessary to cast a vote. They would be outraged, and so would you and I.

To clarify further what I have in mind when I refer to resources, I'm going to invite you to contemplate a fictional scenario.

Say that we are all citizens in a New England town with a traditional town meeting. As usual, a modest proportion of the citizens eligible to attend have actually turned out, let's say four or five hundred.

After calling the meeting to order, the moderator announces:

> "We have established the following rules for this evening's discussion. After a motion has been properly made and seconded, in order to ensure free speech under rules fair to everyone here, each of you who wishes to do so will be allowed to speak on the motion. However, to enable as many as possible to speak, no one will be allowed to speak for more than two minutes."

Perfectly fair so far, you might say. But now our moderator goes on:

> "After everyone who wishes to speak for two minutes has had the floor, each and every one of you is free to speak further, but under one condition. Each additional minute will be auctioned off to the highest bidder."

The ensuing uproar from the assembled citizens would probably drive the moderator and the board of selectman away from the town hall—and perhaps out of town.

Yet isn't this in effect what the Supreme Court decided in the famous case of Buckley v. Valeo? In a seven-to-one vote, the court held that the First Amendment–guarantee of freedom of expression was impermissibly infringed by the limits placed by the Federal Election Campaign Act on the amounts that candidates for federal office or their supporters might spend to promote their election.[3] Well, we've had time to see the appalling consequences.

What went wrong? The justices failed to view campaign expenditures and contributions in the context of a democratic system that derives its legitimacy from the principles of political equality that I described earlier. In order to exercise the fundamental rights to which citizens in a democratic order are entitled—to vote, speak, publish, protest, assemble, organize, among others—citizens must also possess the minimal *resources* that are necessary in order to take advantage of the opportunities and to exercise their rights.

The problem of matching resources to democratic rights admits of no easy answer. Nor can the problem be solved merely by constitutional prescription. But surely a constitution is deeply flawed if the highest court in the land can interpret it to impose an immoveable barrier to the achievement of a satisfactory degree of political equality among its citizens.

A Democratic Role for the Supreme Court

In earlier chapters I alluded to a problem that our best legal and constitutional scholars have disputed at length yet remains with us still. In American constitutional circles it sometimes travels under the name of "the counter-majoritarian difficulty."

I'll put the difficulty this way. We cannot simultaneously lodge the authority to make laws and policies exclusively in the hands of elected officials who are, at least in principle, accountable to citizens through elections and at the same time give the judicial branch the authority, in effect, to make crucial public policies. That dilemma presents us with a difficult choice. Many Americans will resist making it. But if we were ever to undertake a discussion about the adequacy of our constitution when we assess it against democratic standards, this problem, which so far been discussed mainly among legal scholars, would have to be opened up to public debate and discussion.

There is, I believe, an important place in a democratic country for a supreme court with the authority to review the constitutionality of legislative and administrative enactments. For one thing, a federal system needs a high court empowered to decide if and when state authorities have exceeded their proper bounds. But a supreme court should also have the authority to overturn federal laws and administrative decrees that seriously impinge on any of the fundamental rights that are necessary to the existence of a democratic political system: rights to express one's views freely, to assemble, to vote, to form and to participate in political organizations, and so on.[4]

When the court acts within this sphere of fundamental democratic rights, the legitimacy of its actions and its place in the democratic system of government can hardly be challenged. But the more it moves outside this realm—a vast realm in itself—the more dubious its authority becomes. For then it becomes an unelected legislative body. In the guise of interpreting the Constitution—or, even more questionable, divining the obscure and often unknowable intentions of the Framers—the high court enacts important laws and policies that are the proper province of elected officials.

Even within the realm of fundamental democratic rights the decisions of the court will arouse controversy. And controversy is all the more likely because our understanding of democratic rights will surely continue to evolve.

Is Significant Change Possible?

My reflections lead me to a measured pessimism about the prospects for greater democratization of the American Constitution. Changes described in this chapter that would be desirable from a democratic point of view seem to me to have very little chance of coming about in the indefinite future. Although my judgments about likelihoods are necessarily subjective, I believe that most others familiar with American political life would concur.

The likelihood of reducing the extreme *inequality of representation in the Senate* is virtually zero. The chances of altering our constitutional system to make it either *more clearly consensual or more definitely majoritarian* are also quite low. The likelihood is very low that the Supreme Court will refrain from legislating public policies, often highly partisan ones, and instead focus its power of judicial review strictly on the protection of fundamental democratic rights and issues of federalism. The combination of chief executive and monarchy in the American presidency is not likely to change. Finally, the probability that democratic changes in the electoral college will occur appear to be inversely related to their desirability, with the most desirable having the lowest probability of occurring. There is at least a modest chance that some states might require their electoral votes to be allocated in proportion to the popular votes. But a constitutional amendment that makes the number of a state's electors proportionate to its population stands little chance of adoption. And the inequality in representation in the Senate makes a constitutional amendment providing for direct popular election of the president virtually impossible.

Those who regard the Constitution as a sacred icon will, no doubt, take comfort from this conclusion: my pessimism is the mirror image of their optimism.

Yet the historic, if fitful, American impulse toward democracy and political equality has not come to an end. And so, we face a challenge. Given the present limits I have described, how might we advance toward a fuller achievement of democratic processes, rights, liberties, opportunities, and resources?

Let me suggest two very general strategies.

First, it is time—long-past time—to invigorate and greatly widen the critical examination of the Con-

stitution and its shortcomings. Public discussion that
penetrates beyond the Constitution as a national icon
is virtually nonexistent. Even when in-depth analysis
does occur—mainly among constitutional scholars in
schools of law and departments of political science and
history—the Constitution as a whole is rarely tested
against democratic standards or against the performance of constitutional systems in other advanced democratic countries.

I can envision the possibility—here a degree of
optimism breaks through—of a gradually expanding
discussion that begins in scholarly circles, moves out-
ward to the media and intellectuals more generally,
and after some years begins to engage a wider public.
I cannot say what the outcome might be. But surely it
would heighten understanding of the relevance of
democratic ideas to the constitution of a democratic
country, and specifically it would heighten understanding of the shortcomings of the existing constitution
viewed from that perspective and of the possibilities of
change.

Meanwhile, however, we need a second strategy,
one designed to achieve greater *political* equality within
the limits of the present American Constitution. A major
objective of such a strategy would be to reduce the
vast inequalities in the existing distribution of *political
resources*. The characteristics of the Constitution that
I have described in this book will, of course, stand as
obstacles to the success of such a strategy, for they arm
those who possess the greatest resources with strong

defenses—opportunities to veto changes—against all efforts to reduce their privileged positions.

I cannot foresee how successful either strategy may prove to be. But the belief of most Americans that a democratic government, warts and all, is better in the end than any feasible alternative to it is justified on fundamental principles of human equality that cannot be tightly bounded. Our understanding of the implications of those principles will therefore continue to evolve indefinitely. So, too, will the implications of those principles for our democratic political system, and its Constitution, under which we Americans freely choose to live.

CHAPTER 8

Further Reflections:
Changing the Unwritten Constitution

———◆———

BECAUSE SOME OF THE MOST UNDEMOCRATIC features of the Constitution are fixed into that document by provisions that are virtually impossible to alter, at the end of the last chapter I expressed "a measured pessimism" about the prospects for significant change.

Perhaps I was too pessimistic. Changes that would make our *written* constitution more democratic may not be politically feasible. But we could make changes in our *unwritten* constitution much more readily.

The Written and Unwritten American Constitution

I'm aware that the distinction between our formal or written constitution and our informal or unwritten constitution may be puzzling to some of my American readers. Unlike the British, who have lived for centuries with an unwritten constitution that is nowhere laid out in a single document that one could call the British constitution,[1] Americans may find it hard to realize that we are accustomed to certain traditional political practices, institutions, and procedures that we tend to take for granted as essential aspects of our American system of government, even though they are not prescribed by the written constitution.

Of course the written constitution *can* be amended and it has been. In addition to the first ten amendments, which we might reasonably view as part of the original document, from 1798 to 1992 Americans have amended the Constitution seventeen times. Of these, only three, however, had such a distinctive impact on geographical minorities that almost certainly they would have been derailed in the Senate throughout most of the nation's history: the seventy years before the Civil War and the ninety years after the end of Reconstruction in 1876. The decade following the Civil War provided a brief window of opportunity for enacting the Thirteenth, Fourteenth, and Fifteenth Amendments—which were imposed on the defeated Southern states by the victorious North. Of the remaining fourteen amendments, none mobilized widespread opposing interests among the smaller states.

Equal Representation in the Senate = Unequal Representation of Citizens

The Census of 2000, which was completed after my lectures were published, shows that the power to veto constitutional amendments reposes in the hands of an ever tinier geographical minority.

Let's recall that the Constitution requires an amendment to receive two-thirds of the votes cast in the Senate. A proposed amendment can be blocked, then, by the votes of two senators from one-third of the states, plus one additional vote. In the existing Senate composed of two senators from each of the fifty states, thirty-four Senate votes are sufficient to block a constitutional amendment. If an amendment does achieve the necessary number of votes in the Senate, it must then be approved by the legislatures (or, an unused alternative, conventions) in three-fourths of the states; thus it can be blocked by one-fourth of the states plus one more, or thirteen states.

From the Census of 2000 it is easy to calculate that an amendment could be blocked by

thirty-four senators from the seventeen smallest states
with a total population of 20,495,878,
or 7.28 percent of the population of the United States.

If miraculously the amendment were to pass the Senate it could then be blocked by

thirteen state legislatures in the smallest states
with a total population of 10,904,865,
or 3.87 percent of the population of the United States.

The power of a geographical minority of the American populations consists not only in its constitutional ability to veto amendments. In principle, at least, a law could be passed in the Senate by

fifty-one senators from twenty-six states
with a total population of 50,025,674,
or 17.92 percent of the population of the United States.

As I mentioned earlier, Madison and his colleagues vigorously opposed equal representation in the Senate in 1787 at a time when his own state of Virginia, the biggest, was already twelve times larger in population than the smallest, Delaware. Imagine their dismay if they had foreseen the enormity of the difference in 2000, when the largest, California, was nearly seventy times larger than Wyoming, the smallest! If Madison were alive today I have little doubt he would support a constitutional amendment to abolish the electoral college, or at the very least an amendment to reduce the degree of inequality of representation in its composition. But he would immediately discover that no such amendment would be likely to overcome the power of tiny geographical minorities to block constitutional changes by exercising their vetoes in the Senate and the state legislatures.

Does It Really Matter?

A skeptic might reasonably ask, Does this formula for inequality really matter? To begin with, it clearly violates the basic principles that, in my view, are at the foundation of democratic government, provide its legitimacy, and render it, with all its defects, superior to all feasible nondemocratic alternatives. These principles are as follows:

- The principle of *political equality* among citizens.
- The moral judgment that we ought to regard the good of every human being as intrinsically equal to that of another, and therefore in arriving at its decisions the government must give equal consideration to the good and interests of each person.
- A prudential judgment derived from powerful historical evidence about the way groups of people once excluded from full citizenship were treated (for example, women, working classes, poor people, persons without substantial property, African Americans, American Indians). The only reasonable conclusion from this mass of evidence is, I believe, that except on a very strong showing to the contrary in rare circumstances, protected by law, every adult subject to the laws should be considered sufficiently well qualified to participate as a political equal in a democratic process of governing (Dahl, 1998: 62–76; Dahl, 1989, 83–97).[2]

Still, you might wonder whether the formula leads to any practical consequences for public policies. The answer is yes.

Although no comprehensive study of the consequences of equal state representation in the Senate for the passage of legislation over the nation's history seems to have been undertaken, an excellent analysis of some of the more recent effects of the constitutional requirement is provided in a work aptly entitled *Sizing Up the Senate: The Unequal Consequences of Equal Representation* (Lee and Oppenheimer, 1999).

Here we learn that an American who happens to live in a state with a small population automatically gains at least three kinds of political advantages over any citizen who happens to live in a larger state:[3]

- first, as I've already emphasized, the vote of a citizen in a small state counts for more in determining the composition of the Senate than the vote of citizen in a larger state;
- second, this constitutionally ordained political inequality is further exaggerated because the smaller number of citizens in a less populated state enables them to gain much easier access to their senators;
- third, political inequality is exaggerated even further because senators from small states have more time available for activity and even leadership within the Senate itself.

For federal expenditures the consequences are striking. Controlling for other relevant factors, the citizens located in small states are clearly the winners. For example, Wyoming's annual share of federal expenditures is likely to be around $209 per capita compared with California's $132 (Lee and Oppenheimer, 173–76). On what general principle is a citizen living in Wyoming entitled to half again as much in federal funds as a citizen in similar circumstances who is living in California?

Supermajorities: With and Without Principle

A change in laws or constitutional arrangements that requires more than a simple majority—a supermajority—and thereby allows a minority to veto the proposed change seems to contradict a fundamental principle of democratic government: the principle of majority rule. Should the principle of majority rule always be upheld in a democracy? Can supermajorities never be justified on basic democratic principles?

These questions are too profound and difficult for simple answers. The proper place of majority rule and supermajorities in a democratic system presents problems that have been much discussed among democratic theorists, philosophers, and others. Because a responsible response to that complex discussion would far exceed my limits here, I am going to limit myself to five propositions that I believe are necessary assumptions for any fruitful dialogue among those of us who believe in democracy and wish to sustain and advance it, as I assume most of my readers do:

1. A requirement for a supermajority—that is, a minority veto—must be justified by an *explicit principle that is itself justifiable*. So once again: what reasonable principle can justify the unequal representation of citizens in the Senate? Anyone who defends this form of unequal representation is, I believe, obligated to set forth and defend a general principle that will provide an acceptable rationale for such an extreme violation of political equality among American citizens.

2. In rejecting this particular form of minority veto on democratic grounds, we do not thereby imply that a majority is entitled to do whatever it wishes. No majority is morally entitled to infringe on rights, liberties, and opportunities that are essential to the

existence and operation of democracy itself, rights and liberties such as free speech, free, fair, and reasonably frequent elections, freedom of association, and the like. As I argued earlier (153), it is a logical self-contradiction to employ democratic principles and processes to justify an action by a majority that would violate those very principles and processes. To say that a majority is capable of destroying democracy is not to say that a majority is morally entitled to destroy democracy.

3. The interests of geographical minorities can be protected in two ways. The fundamental rights that members of a geographical minority possess as citizens in a democracy can be protected by the legislative and judicial enforcement of existing guarantees in the Bill of Rights and later amendments to the Constitution. In addition, authority to make decisions over matters that are predominantly of local concern can be protected both by statute and by the federal principles built into the existing Constitution.

4. Even though a majority is capable of destroying democracy, the likelihood that it will do so is often greatly exaggerated. I am not aware of any instance of a country where all the essential democratic institutions were fully in place for a generation or more in which a majority has actually decided, by democratic procedures, to replace their democratic system with a nondemocratic regime. Although the fall of the Weimar Republic in 1933 is sometimes offered as an example, the Nazi party never received a majority of votes in a free and fair election.[4] And in any case, at the time of its demise the Weimar Republic had existed for fewer than fifteen years.

5. Although no judicial system could prevent a determined majority, or probably even a determined minority, from destroying democracy, the first two
propositions imply, I believe, that a democratic
constitution might properly endow an independent
court with the power to exercise a veto over laws
and policies that are demonstrably harmful to the
essential institutions of democracy.

Although many Americans are unaware of the fact,
no such judicial veto provision explicitly exists in the
written American Constitution. Nonetheless, the authority of the Supreme Court to overrule laws and
policies that, in its view, violate the Constitution has
become a widely accepted part of our unwritten constitution since 1803, when the Supreme Court first
claimed that authority.

And thereby created an enduring problem. Because the written constitution often provides little
clear-cut guidance, and on many questions the "intentions of the Framers" are highly elusive, unknowable,
or ambiguous, the Supreme Court has often used its
power to impose policies that were little more than reflections of the political ideologies of a majority of
members of the Court (Dahl, 1958; Rosenberg, 2001;
Sandler and Schoenbrod, 2003).

Yet I see little prospect for changing this part of
our unwritten constitution. The Supreme Court will
continue to exist, I expect, as the unelected policy-
making body that it has been since 1803.

Changing the Unwritten Constitution

If the prospects for amending the written constitution to remove its remaining undemocratic features are slight, and the chances for democratizing some aspects of our unwritten constitution, like the policy-making role of the Supreme Court, seem little better, what if any changes in the unwritten constitution might make it more democratic?

One feature of our unwritten constitution that we could alter, and in my view should, is the electoral system (supra, 55–61). Although electoral reform isn't the only democratic innovation that we might want to consider, and perhaps isn't the most consequential, it provides us with an excellent example of possibilities that I believe need to be given serious public discussion and consideration. Fortunately, several recent works provide an excellent foundation for a wider discussion (Thompson, 2002; Hill, 2002; Amy, 2003).

So I'm going to conclude by offering a brief recapitulation of the deficiencies of our existing electoral system and a summary of some feasible alternatives that would be considerably more democratic.

Winner Take All

As I have mentioned (57), perhaps the most obvious consequence of winner-take-all elections is the disproportion—often quite extreme—between the percentage of votes won by a party's candidate and the percentage of seats the party gains in a legislative body.

Defenders of winner-take-all voting often present this disproportion as an advantage: by reinforcing the legislative strength of the winning party, winner take all enables a majority government to carry out its policies more effectively. It is true that a winner-take-all system may be satisfactory for elections that meet two requirements: voters are divided on a single type of policy, such as the economy, and their attitudes are located pretty much along a single dimension, ranging, let us say, from Left to Center to Right, with most voters holding views near the middle. If this were a steady state, then winner-take-all elections would probably result in a competitive two-party system in which almost all voters would support the party that advocates a policy closest to their own views. In this highly idealized situation, the party that wins the election would probably represent the views of a majority of citizens more adequately than the losing party, and its overrepresentation would ensure that it could enact the policies for which a majority of voters had expressed their support.

But this abstract situation is rare. Today, governments affect citizens in so many different ways— taxes, education, the environment, social security, foreign policy, military policy, health, jobs, abortion, human rights, education, housing, transportation, immigration, and many more—that the views of voters don't fall nicely along just one dimension. In this case, a winner-take-all voting system is highly unsatisfactory for many reasons:

- A candidate may win office without receiving a majority of votes. In a three-way race, theoretically a candidate could gain office with just 34 percent of the votes, in a four-way race with only 26 percent, and so on. Though these extreme outcomes are unlikely, winning office without gaining a majority of votes is far from uncommon.

- If the winner has obtained less than 50 percent of the vote, a clear majority of voters might have preferred the candidate who came in second. Thus if the second choices of voters were taken into account, the loser among the two top candidates might instead become the winner, in some cases by a substantial margin.

- In states or districts that are perceived to be preponderantly in favor of one candidate, the incentives to vote are greatly reduced among supporters of all the other candidates. If you know in advance that your vote won't make any difference in the outcome, why vote?

- Citizens who believe that they aren't represented by either of the two major parties may entirely give up on politics and elections. In the extreme case they may become alienated from democracy itself.

- As I pointed out earlier (107–08), winner-take-all elections typically result in a larger number of clearcut losers than proportional systems. Under winner take all, theoretically up to just under half the voters can be losers. In proportional systems, "losers" can still win a share in governing when representatives of their party join a coalition government in which its views are taken into account. In any event, they can reasonably feel that their votes have been fairly weighed in determining the outcome.

- As a result, in proportional systems, "losers" are more inclined to be satisfied with the way democracy works in their country (supra, 108).

Gerrymandering

If election districts are used for choosing representatives to legislative bodies, as Americans do for elections to the House of Representatives and most state legislatures and city councils, it strongly encourages gerrymandering. Designing the boundaries of a district to favor certain candidates over others is an old American practice. (The term *gerrymandering* goes back to 1811, when the governor of Massachusetts, Elbridge Gerry, signed a redistricting bill creating a district shaped so much like a serpent that a newspaper editor promptly announced that it was not a salamander but a Gerrymander.) The result of gerrymandering is the election of a candidate who wins overwhelmingly in a district that has been deliberately shaped to include sympathetic voters and exclude unsympathetic voters.

This rude fact generates a political dynamic:

- Elected politicians naturally have strong incentives to gerrymander the electoral districts in favor of themselves or their party.
- To do so they will, of course, engage in horse trading with elected politicians of the opposing party,

thus guaranteeing that both parties end up with gerrymandered districts that are considered safe for their candidates.

- To keep control of the process of redistricting, elected politicians will try to ensure that they—not an independent commission—are entrusted with the task of designing district boundaries. In 2002 only six states provided for an independent commission. In all the rest, the state legislature had the final say, either directly (in thirty-six states) or by acting as the final authority (in eight states) (Thompson, 173, 242).

- Consequently, after each decennial census the shape of the state's districts is determined in most state legislatures by an unseemly round of partisan strong arming, bickering, bargaining, and log rolling—as anyone could have observed after the census of 2000.

- The upshot is that safe seats are created and the number of potentially competitive districts is reduced. Partisan redistricting after the 2000 census led to an election in 2002 in which only thirty-five to forty seats in the House of Representatives were competitive.[5] Gerrymandering ensured that all the rest, nearly nine out of ten, had been rendered safe for one party or the other.

As a result, even our House of Representatives may not always be very representative.

Alternatives to Winner Take All

As I noted earlier, with only two exceptions, Britain and Canada, all the other mature democracies employ an alternative to winner take all. Because the various alternatives are too many to describe, I'll briefly mention only a few of the possibilities with which I think Americans should be more familiar.[6]

If no candidate receives more than 50 percent of the vote, a *runoff* (or *second round*) election takes place between the two candidates with the largest number of votes. This system is used in France for elections to the parliament and the presidency. Its main disadvantage is the additional time, effort, and money it requires; in the United States, with our acute problem of campaign finance, this would be especially problematic.

This drawback could be removed, however, by *preferential voting,* (sometimes called an *instant runoff*). Although preferential voting has many variations, basically it allows or requires voters to rank the candidates in the order of their preferences. Here is one advocate's description: "If no candidate receives more than 50 percent of the initial vote, the candidate with the fewest votes is eliminated and his votes transferred to the candidates designated as the second choice on these ballots. This process of elimination and transfer goes on until one candidate receives more than 50 percent of the vote" (Thompson, 71).

A system along these lines has been used in Australia since 1901 and in Ireland since 1922.

Another alternative is *proportional representation (PR),* an electoral system that ensures a strong relation between the percentage of votes cast for a party and the percentage of parliamentary seats a party wins. Among the twenty-two advanced democracies, more employ PR than any other electoral system (see table 3, p. 166).

PR Plus Single-Member Districts

In many countries that use PR, voters don't have an opportunity to elect a candidate to represent their own district. Most Americans would probably view this as a drawback.

However, *PR can be combined with single-member districts*. Here is how it might work in the United States. For illustrative purposes, let's assume a House of Representatives with 600 seats rather than the present 435. Half of these seats would be filled by elections held in 300 congressional districts, in each of which the single seat would be won, as it is now, in a winner-take-all election. Voters would also cast a second vote, however, for a *list* of statewide candidates nominated by the voter's preferred *party*. These would be allocated so that the percentage of each party's seats in the House would closely match the percentage of votes it received in the election. Thus if one party wins 40 percent of the national vote for members of Congress, but gains only 20 percent of the total House seats in the district elections, enough candidates from the national list would then be added to match the party's percentage of House seats with its percentage of the national vote. A party with, say, 40 percent of the national votes could expect to gain about 40 percent of the seats in the House.

Because this system combines the advantages of district elections with the fairness of proportionality, some observers regard it as the best of both worlds. It has been used in Germany since the Federal Republic was inaugurated in 1949, and in 1993 it replaced winner take all in New Zealand. In Italy it is used for elections to both chambers of parliament, though in a country in which dissatisfaction with electoral systems is more endemic, it also evokes a considerable amount of criticism and proposals for change.

Some Words of Caution, Some Words of Hope

Lest we expect too much, let me now append a few words of caution. First, as with a great many, perhaps most, political choices, as best I can judge no electoral system is entirely without some drawbacks. Second, as with other political institutions, an electoral system that works well in one country may be less satisfactory in another. Third, then, an electoral system should be designed to meet the conditions of a particular country—in the case we're considering, the United States.[7]

And some words of hope.

Nearly a century ago a distinguished Supreme Court Justice, Louis Brandeis, argued that the states provide an accessible testing ground for possible changes. Indeed, some of the most important amendments to the Constitution—abolition of slavery, direct election of senators, women's suffrage—first gained acceptance at the state level, where they helped to build up a powerful national constituency that ultimately prevailed. Possibilities can also be tried out at the municipal level.

As I said earlier, our winner-take-all electoral system is only one undemocratic legacy that we need to confront. Other undemocratic features of our unwritten Constitution are also open to change.

Most Americans would probably agree that the basic *rights* necessary to democratic institutions should be fairly distributed among our citizens. But as I pointed out in the previous chapter, democratic principles also require a fair distribution of *opportunities* to act on those rights and the *political resources* necessary if citizens are to be able to take advantage of the opportunities. Yet we have barely begun to explore ways to reduce the huge disparities in the political resources that citizens require if they are to participate more effectively in campaigns, elections, and influencing policy. For example, despite recent and very hard-fought changes, the way that electoral campaigns are financed still remains an egregious failure to meet elementary democratic standards.

★   ★   ★

CONTRARY TO A BELIEF WIDELY HELD AMONG AMERIcans, our great and enduring gift to the world was not our Constitution, which was little imitated and indeed largely rejected as a model among the successful and enduring democratic countries that would emerge in the next century. No, far greater were two other gifts.

One was the demonstration by Americans that among a relatively free and independent people a *written constitution* prescribing the political structures of a democratic republic could be designed, ratified, occasionally amended, and sufficiently respected among political leaders and ordinary citizens to endure indefinitely. Even if the specific features of the American Constitution failed to serve as a model for other countries that would successfully pursue their own paths toward a stable democracy, the United States offered living proof for all the world to see that a written constitution could help to create and maintain the durable structures needed for a representative democracy.

Yet a greater gift, I believe, was what foreign travelers like Alexis de Tocqueville observed and reported to Europe and beyond: to a degree that had hitherto been thought far beyond mortal reach, the idea and the ideals of democracy and political equality could profoundly shape political life, beliefs, culture, and institutions in a huge, growing, diverse, progressive, and prosperous country.

Constitution
&
equality

On the Terms "Democracy" and "Republic"

———————◆·◆———————

THE VIEW THAT THE FRAMERS INTENDED TO create a republic, not a democracy, probably has its origins in comments by Madison in Federalist No. 10. Although there as elsewhere he also used the expression "popular government" as a kind of generic term, he distinguished further between "a pure democracy, by which I mean a society consisting of a small number of persons, who assemble and administer the government in person," and a "republic, by which I mean a government in which the scheme of representation takes place." "The two great points of difference between a democracy and a republic are: first, the delegation of the government, in the latter, to a small number of citizens elected by the rest; secondly, the greater number of citizens, and greater

sphere of the country, over which the latter may be extended."[1]

Here Madison was making the common distinction
that political scientists and others would later differen-
tiate as "direct democracy" and "representative democracy." For it was as evident to the Framers as it is
to us that given the size of a nation composed of the
thirteen existing states, with more to come, "the
people" could not possibly assemble directly to enact
laws, as they did at the time in New England town
meetings and had done two millennia earlier in Greece,
where the term "democracy" was invented. It was perfectly obvious to the Framers, then, that in such a
large country, a republican government would have to
be a *representative* government, where national laws
would be enacted by a representative legislative body
consisting of members chosen directly or indirectly by
the people.

Madison was probably also influenced by a long
tradition of "republicanism" that in both theory and
practice leaned somewhat more toward aristocracy, limited suffrage, concern for property rights, and fear of
the populace than toward a broadly based popular government more dependent on "the will of the people."

It is also true, however, that during the eighteenth
century the terms "democracy" and "republic" were
used rather interchangeably in both common and
philosophical usage.[2] Madison, in fact, was well aware
of the difficulty of defining "republic." In Federalist
No. 39, he posed the question "What, then, are the

distinctive characters (sic) of the republican form?" In response he pointed to the enormous range of meanings given to the word "republic." "Were an answer to this question to be sought . . . in the application of the term by political writers, to the constitutions of different states, no satisfactory one could ever be found. Holland, in which no particle of the supreme authority is derived from the people, has passed almost universally under the denomination of a republic. The same title has been bestowed on Venice, where absolute power over the great body of the people is exercised, in the most absolute manner, by a small body of hereditary nobles."

In view of this ambiguity, Madison proposed that "we may define a republic to be . . . a government which derives all its powers directly or indirectly from the great body of the people, and is administered by persons holding their offices during pleasure, or for a limited period, or during good behavior."[3] By defining a republic as a government which derives all its powers "*directly* or indirectly from the great body of the people," Madison now seems to be contradicting the distinction he had drawn earlier in Federalist No. 10. We might read his struggle with definitions as a further illustration of the prevailing confusion over the two terms.

If further evidence were needed of the ambiguity of terminology, we could turn to a highly influential writer whose work was well known to Madison and many of his contemporaries. In *The Spirit of the Laws*

(1748) Montesquieu had distinguished three kinds of governments: republican, monarchic, and despotic. Republican governments were of two kinds: "When, in a republic, the people as a body have the sovereign power, it is a *Democracy*. When the sovereign power is in the hands of a part of the people, it is called an *Aristocracy*."[4] But Montesquieu also insisted that "It is in the nature of a republic that it has only a small territory: without that it could scarcely exist."[5]

From Aristotle to Montesquieu, political philosophers had no place in their classifications for *representative* democracy. It was simply an unknown species, one yet to evolve. In November 1787, however, only two months after the Philadelphia convention had adjourned, James Wilson had already updated the older classifications:

"The three species of governments . . . are the monarchical, aristocratical and democratical. In a monarchy, the supreme power is vested in a single person: in an aristocracy . . . by a body not formed upon the principle of representation, but enjoying their station by descent, or election among themselves, or in right of some personal or territorial qualifications; and lastly, in a democracy, *it is inherent in a people, and is exercised by themselves or their representatives* [italics added]. . . . [O]f what description is the Constitution before us? In its principles, Sir, it is purely democratical: varying indeed in its form in order to admit all the advantages, and to exclude all the disadvantages which are incidental to the known and established constitution of government. But when we take an extensive and accurate view of the streams of power that appear through this great and comprehensive plan . . . we shall be able to trace them to one great and noble source, THE PEOPLE."[6] At the Virginia ratifying convention ome month later, John Marshall, the future chief justice of the Supreme Court, declared that the "Constitution provided for 'a well regulated democracy' where no king, or president, could undermine representative government."[7]

Although the Framers differed among themselves as to how democratic they wanted their republic to be,[8] for obvious reasons they were of one mind about the need for a representative government. But as events soon showed, they could not fully determine just how democratic that representative government would become—under the leadership of, among others, James Madison.

Appendix B

Tables and Figures

TABLE 1. Countries Steadily Democratic Since at Least 1950

1. Austria
2. Australia
3. Belgium
4. Canada
5. Costa Rica
6. Denmark
7. Finland
8. France
9. Germany
10. Iceland
11. Ireland
12. Israel
13. Italy
14. Japan
15. Luxembourg
16. Netherlands
17. New Zealand
18. Norway
19. Sweden
20. Switzerland
21. United Kingdom
22. United States

Note: The countries are broken down as follows: *European:* Austria, Belgium, Denmark, Finland, France, Germany, Iceland, Ireland, Italy, Luxembourg, Netherlands, Norway, Sweden, Switzerland, United Kingdom (15); *English-speaking:* Australia, New Zealand, United Kingdom, United States (4); *Latin American:* Costa Rica; *other:* Israel, Japan. Although India gained independence in 1947, adopted a democratic constitution, and has, except for one interval, maintained its democratic institutions in the face of extraordinary challenges of poverty and diversity, I have omitted it from the list for two reasons. First, continuity was interrupted from 1975 to 1977 when the prime minister, Indira Gandhi, staged a coup d'état, declared a state of emergency, suspended civil rights, and imprisoned thousands of opponents. Second, because India is one of the poorest countries in the world, comparisons with the wealthy countries in Table 5 would make little sense.

TABLE 2. How the U.S. Constitutional-Political System Compares with the Other 21 Older Democracies

| Characteristics of the U.S. system | Among the other 21 countries, those that are similar in this respect | |
	(n)	Countries
Federalism		
1. *Strong federalism*	6	Austria, Australia, Canada, Germany, Switzerland, Belgium
2. *Strongly bicameral legislature*	3	All federal: Australia, Germany, Switzerland
3. *Significant unequal representation in the upper house*	4	All federal: Australia, Canada, Germany, Switzerland
Non-Federal Features		
4. *Strong judicial review of national legislation*	2	Canada, Germany
5. *Electoral system: plurality elections in single member districts (FPTP)*	2	Britain, Canada
6. *Strong two-party system; third parties weak*[1]	3	Australia[2], New Zealand,[3] Costa Rica
7. *Presidential system: single popularly elected chief executive with important constitutional powers*		None

[1] Until the 1997 election, held under the new PR system, when the two major parties received only 61% of the vote. The rest was split almost entirely among three minor parties.

[2] Where the total vote cast for third party candidates is ordinarily under 10% of the total.

[3] Until 2000, counting the Liberal National (earlier Liberal-Country) coalition as one party.

TABLE 3.   The Electoral Systems of the Advanced
Democracies

PR: List System	PR: Variants	Plurality in SingleMember Districts (FPTP)	Variant
1. Austria	1. Australia (AV)	1. Canada	France
2. Belgium	2. Germany (MMP)	2. United Kingdom	(2 rounds)
3. Costa Rica	3. Ireland (STV)	3. United States	
4. Denmark	4. Italy (MMP)		
5. Finland	5. Japan (semi PR)		
6. Iceland	6. New Zealand (MMP)		
7. Israel			
8. Luxembourg			
9. Netherlands			
10. Norway			
11. Sweden			
12. Switzerland			

Source: Andrew Reynolds and Ben Reilly, *The International IDEA Handbook of Electoral System Design* (1997)

Note: AV = Alternative Vote; MMP = Multimember Proportional; STV = Single Transferable Vote.

TABLE 4.   Proportionality vs. Majoritarianism:
20 Democratic Countries

Predominantly Proportional	Mixed	Predominantly Majoritarian
Austria	Ireland	Australia
Belgium	Japan	Canada
Denmark	*Spain*	France
Finland	USA	*Greece*
Germany		New Zealand (to 1993)
Netherlands		United Kingdom
New Zealand (1993)		
Norway		
Sweden		
Switzerland		

Source: Powell, *Elections as Instruments of Democracy* (2000), p. 41. I have changed his table to show the adoption of proportionality in New Zealand in 1993.

Note: The list is slightly different from Table 1. It includes Spain and Greece, democratized since 1950, and it does not include Costa Rica, Iceland, Israel, or Luxembourg.

TABLE 5.   Measures of U.S. Performance among
Democratic Countries

Variable	U.S. Rank	No. of Countries	Percentage of Countries Performing Better than U.S.[1]
U.S. in BEST third			
Economic growth, 1980–95	5th best (tied) of	18	24
U.S. in MIDDLE third			
Women's cabinet representation, 1993–95	8th most of	22	33
Popular support for executive, 1945–96[2]	10th most of	22	43
Budget deficits, 1970–95	8th highest (tied) of	16	47
Unemployment, 1971–95[3]	8th highest (tied) of	18	59
Family policy, 1976–82	12th best of	18	65
Inflation (CPI), 1970–95	12th highest of	18	65

U.S. in WORST third			
Women's parliamentary representation, 1971–95	18th lowest (tied) of	22	81
Rich-poor ratio, 1981–93	4th greatest of	18	82
Energy efficiency, 1990–94	19th lowest of	22	86
Welfare state index, 1980	17th lowest of	18	94
Social expenditures, 1992	17th lowest of	18	94
Voter turnout, 1971–96	21st lowest of	22	95
Incarceration rate, 1992–95	1st highest of	18	100
Foreign aid, 1992–95	19th lowest of	19	100

Source: I am indebted to Arend Lijphart for his permission to use the data set he developed for *Patterns of Democracy* (New Haven: Yale University Press, 1999) where the variables and their sources are described. I also owe thanks to Jennifer Smith for her contributions to the construction of the table.

[1] The percentages are those of countries scoring better than the United States, and not tied. Variables for which the higher the ranking, the worse a country's performance are in italics.

[2] "The average percentage of the voters who gave their votes to the party or parties that formed the cabinet, or in presidential systems, the percentage of voters who voted for the winning presidential candidate, weighted by the time each cabinet or president was in office." Lijphart 1999, p. 290.

[3] Unstandardized.

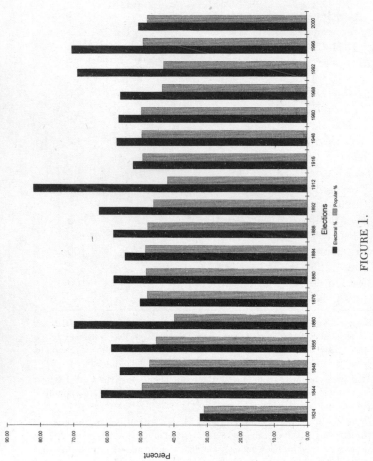

FIGURE 1.

Presidential Elections Won with Less Than 50% of the Popular Vote

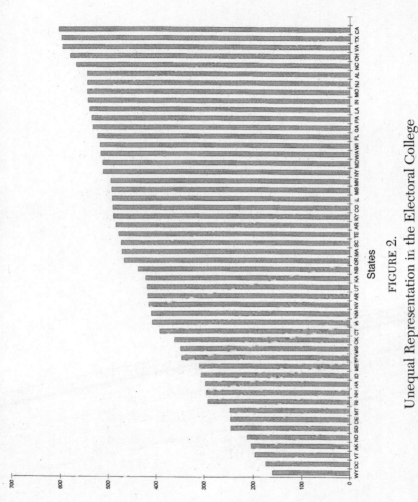

FIGURE 2.

Unequal Representation in the Electoral College

Notes

CHAPTER 1. *Introduction*

1. Although in three states—Delaware, New Jersey, and Georgia—the vote was unanimous, in the rest it was divided, sometimes closely after sharp debate. For example, in Massachusetts the delegates split 187 to 168; in New Hampshire, 57 to 47; in Virginia, 87 to 79. The closest vote was in New York, where the supporters of the Constitution won by three votes.

2. In the ten states where the Convention vote was not unanimous, a total of 1540 delegates voted on the Constitution, 964 for, and 576 against.

CHAPTER 2. *What the Framers Couldn't Know*

1. I quote here from the Journal of the Convention, in Max Farrand, ed., *The Records of the Federal Convention of 1787,* 3 vols. (New Haven: Yale University Press, 1966), 1: 1. The three volumes edited by Farrand were reprinted in 1987 with a fourth volume, a *Supplement* edited by James H. Hutson

(New Haven: Yale University Press, 1987). My references to the records of the Convention are drawn from these four volumes and are cited hereafter as *Records.*

2. William Miller, *The Business of May Next: James Madison and the Founding* (Charlottesville: University Press of Virginia, 1992), 41ff. Lance Banning writes that "Madison had come to Philadelphia the best prepared of all who gathered for the Federal Convention. . . . He first prepared elaborate research notes on the histories and structures of other ancient and modern confederacies." 115.

3. *Records,* 1: 425.

4. Madison took extensive notes during the Convention, which he later edited and also collated with the very brief Journal of the Convention, published in 1819. His notes were published posthumously in 1840. These form a part of the series described in note 1, above. I have maintained Madison's punctuation and spelling.

5. His speech on June 18 as reported by Madison is in *Records,* 1: 282ff. Hamilton said that "he had no scruple in declaring . . . that the British Govt. was the best in the world. . . . As to the Executive, it seemed to be admitted that no good one could be established on Republican principle. . . . The English model was the only good one on this subject." 288, 299.

6. In order to serve as a check on the popular chamber of the national legislature, the second chamber "must have great personal property, it must have the aristocratic spirit; it must love to lord it thro' pride. . . . The aristocratic body, should be as independent & firm as the democratic. . . . To make it independent, it should be for life." Ibid., 1: 512. With his usual admiration for the British system, in his first speech to the Convention, Hamilton opined that the "House of Lords is a most noble institution. Having nothing to hope for by a change, and sufficient interest by means of their property, in being faithful to the National interest, they form a permanent barrier agst. every pernicious innovation." 1: 288 (June 18).

7. A few delegates favored the idea of somehow getting rid of the states and consolidating power in the national government. George Read of Delaware "disliked the idea of guaranteeing territory. It abetted the idea of distinct States wch.

would be a perpetual source of discord. There can be [no] cure for this evil but in doing away with States altogether and uniting them all into [one] great Society." *Records*, 1: 202 (June 11). He had made a similar proposal a few days earlier, on June 6. 136–37. In his maiden address cited above, Hamilton proposed that "the Governor or president of each state shall be appointed by the General Government and shall have a negative upon the laws about to be passed in the State of which he is Governor or President" 293.

8. *Records*, 1: 466.

9. *Records*, 1: 492–93. I have put these remarks in the first person. In Madison's published notes they are recorded in the third person.

10. The advocates of equal representation in the House were defeated on June 29 by a vote of six states for and four states against, with one state (Maryland) divided. Their proposal for equality in the Senate was stalemated by a tie vote on July 2 (five to five, with Georgia divided) and finally carried on July 7 with six voting yes, three voting no, and two states (Massachusetts and Georgia) divided. *Records*, 1: 549.

11. Article I, Section 9. For an excellent account of the only full public debate over the slavery issue, see Joseph J. Ellis, *Founding Brothers: The Revolutionary Generation* (New York: Alfred A. Knopf, 2000), 81–119. The debate took place in the House of Representatives in March 1790 in response to petitions from Quakers in New York and Philadelphia "calling for the federal government to put an immediate end to the African slave trade." (81).

12. Article IV, Section 2.

13. Article I, Sections 2, 3.

14. For a magisterial study of the evolution of American citizenship, see Rogers Smith, *Civic Ideals: Conflicting Visions of Citizenship in U.S. History* (New Haven: Yale University Press, 1997). On the constitution's omission of citizenship for women, Native Americans, and African Americans, see 130–34.

15. Article I, Section 3.

16. By the same electorate as that for "the most numerous branch of the state legislature." (Article I, Section 2).

17. *Records*, 2: 83.

18. For evidence that the Supreme Court sometimes plays such a role, see my "Decision-Making in a Democracy: The Supreme Court as a National Policy-Maker," *Journal of Public Law* 6, no. 2, 279–95.

19. It is only fair to point out that given the political opposition to any increase in federal powers, the Framers may well have gone as far as they could go. Their major opponents, the Anti-Federalists, who saw the constitution as a threat to popular government at the state level, objected that the powers of Congress to regulate interstate commerce were excessive. Richard L. Perry, ed., *The Sources of Our Liberties: Documentary Origins of Individual Liberties in the United States Constitution and Bill of Rights* (New York: American Bar Association, 1959), 240.

20. For an account of the development in the American colonies of ideas and practices concerning popular government, see Edmund S. Morgan, *Inventing the People: The Rise of Popular Sovereignty in England and America* (New York: W. W. Norton, 1988), esp. Chs. 8 and 9, 174–233.

21. Gordon S. Wood, *The Radicalism of the American Revolution* (New York: Alfred A. Knopf, 1992), 230.

22. The numbers are a matter of uncertainty. In some colonies the suffrage may have grown more restricted during the colonial period. "What is also unclear is just how many people could and did vote. This issue is a source of controversy among historians, some of whom conclude that colonial America was a land of middle class democracy in which 80 or 80 percent of all adult white males were enfranchised, while others depict a far more oligarchic and exclusive political order. In fact, enfranchisement varied greatly by location. There certainly were communities, particularly newly settled communities where land was inexpensive, in which 70 or 80 percent of all white men were enfranchised. Yet there were also locales . . . where the percentages were far lower, closer to 40 or 50 percent. Levels of enfranchisement seem to have been higher in New England and in the South (especially Virginia and the Carolinas) than they were in the mid-Atlantic colonies (especially New York, Pennsylvania, and Maryland; not surprisingly, they also tended to be higher in newer settle-

ments than in more developed areas. On the whole, the franchise was far more widespread than it was in England; yet as the revolution approached, the rate of property ownership was falling, and the proportion of adult white males who were eligible to vote was probably less than 60 percent." Alexander Keyssar, *The Right to Vote: The Contested History of Democracy in the United States* (New York: Basic Books, 2000), 7.

23. On the constitution's exclusion of women, Native Americans, and African Americans, see Keyssar, 130–34.

24. *Democracy in America*, trans. Henry Reeve (New York: Schocken, 1961), 1: lxvii.

25. Although Jefferson and his followers often referred to their political group as "Republican," their party seems to have taken the name "Democratic Republican" as early as 1796, and it retained the name through the election of 1828. In 1820, Monroe ran as a Democratic Republican and Adams as an Independent Democratic Republican. In 1824 all four candidates—Adams, Jackson, Crawford, and Clay—ran as factions of the Democratic-Republican party. In 1828, Jackson ran as a Democratic Republican, Adams as a National-Republican. In 1832, Jackson ran as the candidate of the Democratic Party and Clay as a National-Republican. Congressional Quarterly, *Presidential Elections Since 1789*, 2nd ed. (Washington, D.C.: Congressional Quarterly, 1979), 19–27.

26. Joyce Appleby, *Inheriting the Revolution: The First Generation of Americans* (Cambridge, Mass.: Harvard University Press, 2000), 65.

27. "When land offices opened on the frontier, land sales soared. In 1800 some 67,000 acres passed into private hands; 497,939 acres did so in 1801. By 1815 annual sales hit one and a half million dollars, more than doubling four years later." Appleby, *Inheriting the Revolution*, 64. As Gordon Wood remarks in his review, "Tens of thousands of ordinary folk pulled up stakes in the East and moved westward, occupying more territory in a single generation than had been occupied in the 150 years of colonial history." "Early American Get-up-and-Go," *New York Review*, June 29, 2000, 50.

28. For a rather unsympathetic portrait, see Stanley Elkins and Eric McKitrick, *The Age of Federalism: The Early Ameri-*

can Republicanism, 1788–1900 (New York: Oxford University Press, 1993), 706ff.

29. Dubious as one might be—and I am profoundly doubtful—about the contemporary relevance of the Second Amendment securing "the right of the people to keep and bear Arms," I have no doubt that contemporaries saw it as important to maintaining their liberty from a potentially dangerous central government.

30. *Democracy and the Amendments to the Constitution* (Lexington, Mass.: Lexington Books, 1978), 166.

31. *The Federalist* (New York: Modern Library, n.d.), 53ff.

32. The often murky maneuvers preceding the compromise are described in Bernard A. Weisberger, *America Afire: Jefferson, Adams, and the Revolutionary Election of 1800* (New York: William Morrow, 2000), 258–77.

33. Elkins and McKitrick, 263 et seq.

34. Quoted, ibid., 267.

35. *Records,* 3: 452–55. Italics added. Spelling and punctuation as in the original.

36. *The Forging of American Federalism: Selected Writings of James Madison,* Saul K. Padover, ed. (New York: Harper Torchbooks, 1953), letter to Thomas Ritchie, 1825, 46.

37. Marvin Meyers, ed., *The Mind of the Founder: Sources of the Political Thought of James Madison* (New York: Bobbs-Merrill, 1973), 520.

38. Ibid., 523, 525, 530.

CHAPTER 3. *The Constitution as a Model: An American Illusion*

1. In a 1997 survey, 34% strongly agreed and 33% somewhat agreed with the statement "The U.S. Constitution is used as a model by many countries." Only 18% somewhat or strongly disagreed. (Nationwide telephone survey of 1,000 adult U.S. Citizens conducted for the National Constitution Center, September, 1997.) To the statement "I am proud of the U.S. Constitution," 71% strongly agreed and 18% somewhat agreed. In 1999, 85% said the Constitution was a major reason for America's success in the twentieth century. (Survey

of 1,546 adults for the Pew Research Center by the Princeton Survey Research Associates.)

2. Although India gained independence in 1947, adopted a democratic constitution, and has, except for one interval, maintained its democratic institutions in the face of extraordinary challenges of poverty and diversity, I have omitted it from the list for two reasons. First, continuity was interrupted from 1975 to 1977 when the prime minister, Indira Gandhi, staged a coup d'etat, declared a state of emergency, suspended civil rights, and imprisoned thousands of opponents. Second, because India is one of the poorest countries in the world, comparisons with the wealthy democratic countries would make little sense.

3. For a summary of the constitutional differences among twenty-two older democracies, see Appendix B, Table 2.

4. Plus six half-cantons.

5. Robert Hazell and David Sinclair, "The British Constitution: Labour's Constitutional Revolution," *Annual Review of Political Science*, 3 (Palo Alto: Annual Reviews, 2000), 379–400, 393.

6. For example, in the Prussian elections of 1858, 4.8% of the inhabitants were entitled to one-third of the seats, 13.4% to another third, and 81.8% to the remaining third. Thus members of the wealthiest third in effect possessed 17 times as many votes as members of the bottom third. Bernhard Vogel and Rainer-Olaf Schultze, "Deutschland," in *Die Wahl Der Parlamente*, Dolf Sternberger and Bernard Vogel, eds. (Berlin: Walter De Gruyter, 1969), 189–411, Tabelle A 4, p. 348.

7. Lest you think me biased against Nevada, the Rocky Mountain states, or small states in general: I have the greatest affection for Alaska, where I grew up in the days when it was still a territory, and for the Rocky Mountain states, where I like to spend some time every summer. And at just over 3 million people, Connecticut gives me a wholly undeserved voting advantage of nine to one over my sons in California.

8. Alfred Stepan, "Toward a New Comparative Analysis of Democracy and Federalism: Demos Constraining and Demos Enabling Federations," paper for the meeting of the International Political Science Association, Seoul, Aug. 17–22, 1997.

9. For a comprehensive description, analysis, and critique

of unequal representation in the Senate, see Francis E. Lee and Bruce I. Oppenheimer, *Sizing Up the Senate: The Unequal Consequences of Unequal Representation* (Chicago: University Chicago Press, 1999).

10. Stepan, supra n. 8.

11. More precisely, a governmental unit of a "State" defined as a territorial system with a government that successfully upholds a claim to the exclusive regulation of the legitimate use of physical force in enforcing its rules within a given territorial area.

12. For Mason, see *Records*, 1: 483; for Madison, see 447-48.

13. Barry R. Weingast, "Political Stability and Civil War: Institutions, Commitment, and American Democracy," in Robert H. Bates, Avner Greif, Margaret Levi, Jean-Laurent Rosenthal, and Barry R. Weingast, *Analytic Narratives* (Princeton: Princeton University Press, 1988), 148-93, 166, and Table 4.3, 168.

14. Article II, Section 4 provides: "The times, places, and manner of holding elections for Senators and Representatives, shall be prescribed in each State by the Legislature thereof; but the Congress may at any time by Law make or alter such regulations, except as to the place of choosing Senators." Article II, Section 1 provides: "Each state shall appoint, in such manner as the legislature therefore may direct, a number of Electors."

15. Robert Hazell and David Sinclair, "The British Constitution: Labour's Constitutional Revolution," in Nelson W. Polsby, ed., *Annual Review of Political Science,* vol. 3 (Palo Alto: Annual Reviews, 2000), 379-400, 382-85, 391.

16. Lani Guanier, "No Two Seats: The Elusive Quest for Political Equality," *Virginia Law Review* 77 (1991).

17. Maurice Duverger, *Political Parties: Their Organization and Activity in the Modern State* (New York: John Wiley, 1954), 217.

18. In an appraisal of Duverger's propositions in 1958, John Grumm observed that "it may be more accurate to conclude that proportional representation is a result rather than a cause of the party system in a given country." "Theories of Electoral

Systems," *Midwest Journal of Political Science* 2 (1958): 357–76, 375.

19. Arend Lijphart, *Patterns of Democracy, Government Forms and Performance in Thirty-Six Countries* (New Haven: Yale University Press, 1999) uses ten variables to distinguish "majoritarian" from "consensus" democracies. Table 14.1, p. 245. G. Bingham Powell, *Elections as Instruments of Democracy, Majoritarian and Proportional Visions* (New Haven: Yale University Press, 2000) uses the terms of his title: "majoritarian" and "proportional." See pp. 20ff and the classification of twenty democratic countries on p. 41.

20. *Records,* 1: 288, 299.

21. Madison's notes, published in 1840 after his death. See above, note 4.

22. The only delegate recorded by Madison as speaking favorably about the British monarchy was Hamilton. See note 3 above. Ironically, the Federalist Papers defending the provisions of the Constitution on the executive—Nos. 67–77—were by Hamilton.

23. In what follows I have drawn freely from my *Pluralist Democracy in the United States* (Chicago: Rand McNally, 1967), 85ff.

24. A convenient source for some of the relevant discussions is Richard J. Ellis, ed., *Founding the American Presidency* (Lanham, Md.: Rowman and Littlefield, 1999), Ch. 3, 63–96.

25. For a critical view, see my "The Myth of the Presidential Mandate," *Political Science Quarterly* 105, no. 3 (Fall 1990): 355–72.

CHAPTER 4. *Electing the President*

1. For an excellent and much fuller account of the electoral college than brevity permits me here, see Lawrence Longley and Neal R. Peirce, *The Electoral College Primer* (New Haven: Yale University Press, 1999). See also Robert M. Hardaway, *The Electoral College and the Constitution: The Case for Preserving Federalism* (Westport, CT: Praeger, 1994).

2. *Records,* 2: 501.

3. "James Wilson's Final Summation and Rebuttal," December 11, 1787, in *The Debate on the Constitution,* Bernard Bailyn, ed. , 2 vols, Vol. 1, 849.

4. *Records,* 2: 497.

5. *Records,* 2: 522.

6. *The Federalist* (New York: Modern Library, n.d.), 441. Although the other members of the New York delegation had withdrawn from the Convention in June, Hamilton stayed on, though he rarely intervened in the debates and seems to have little influence on the outcome.

7. Ibid., 443.

8. My interpretation of "anxious."

9. *Records,* 2: 500. A fear of "cabal" had been frequently expressed throughout the earlier discussions.

10. Article II provided that "The Person having the greatest Number of [electoral] Votes shall be the President," and "after the choice of the President, the Person having the greatest Number of Votes of the Electors shall be the Vice President."

11. "How could the framers have made such an elementary and colossal blunder? No less puzzling, why did the opponents of the Constitution, who were generally so eager to seize on the document's weaknesses, never once expose this weakness in the mechanics of the electoral college? The short answer is that neither supporters nor opponents of the Constitution anticipated the formation of organized national political parties." Richard J. Ellis, ed., *Founding the American Presidency* (Lanham, Md.: Rowman and Littlefield, 1999), 114.

12. It also provided that if no candidate received a majority of electoral votes, the House would choose among the top three (not five as in the original article).

13. The classic account is by C. Vann Woodward, *Reunion and Reaction: The Compromise of 1877 and the End of Reconstruction* (Boston: Little, Brown: 1951).

14. Congressional Quarterly, *Presidential Elections Since 1789,* 2nd ed. (Washington, D.C.: Congressional Quarterly, 1979), 11.

15. Ellis, 118.

16. The figures may change slightly when the House seats are reapportioned to conform to the 2000 census figures.

17. Ellis, 118.

18. Ibid., 119.

19. For a more extended examination of possibilities for reform, see Lawrence D. Longley and Alan G. Braun, *The Politics of Electoral College Reform,* foreword by U.S. Senator Birch Bayh, 2nd ed. (New Haven, Yale University Press, 1975).

20. The need for a second election could be avoided by means of an electoral system various called Instant Run-off, Alternative Vote (AV), or Preferential Voting. "[U]nder AV electors rank the candidates in the order of their choice by marking '1' for their favorite candidate, '2' for their second-choice, '3' for their third choice, and so on. . . . [A] candidate who has won an absolute majority of votes (50% plus one) is immediately elected. However, if no candidate has an absolute majority, under AV the candidate with the lowest number of preferences is 'eliminated' from the count, and his or her . . . second preferences . . . are then assigned to the remaining candidates in the order as marked on the ballot. This process is repeated until one candidate has an absolute majority, and is declared duly elected." Andrew Reynolds and Ben Reilly, *The International IDEA Handbook of Electoral System Design* (Stockholm: International IDEA, 1997), 38. This system is used in Australia for electing members of parliament in single-member districts. Since 1922 an analogous system—the Single Transferable Vote (STV)—has been used in the Republic of Ireland for the election of members of parliament. However, unlike the presidential elections in the U.S. and parliamentary elections in Australia, in Ireland the members of parliament are elected in districts returning three, four, or five members. The STV system produces a high degree of proportionality between the size of a party's votes and the number of its M.P.s. (Ibid., 85ff).

21. A Gallup survey in 1968 asked respondents, "Would you approve or disapprove of an amendment to the Constitution which would do away with the Electoral College and base the election of the President on the total vote throughout the nation?" Eighty-one per cent approved, 12 percent disap-

proved, and seven percent had no opinion. Longley and Braun, 154. In a 1992 survey, respondents were presented with the statement that "If Perot runs, there is a chance that no presidential candidate will get enough electoral votes to win. If that happens, the Constitution gives the House of Representatives the power to decide who will be the next President. Do you think that is a fair way to choose the President, or should the Constitution be changed." Only 31% felt it was a fair way, while 61% answered that the Constitution should be changed. CBS News-New York Times national telephone survey of 1,346 adults, July, 1992. Another survey in 1992 indicated that Americans were far from agreed on how their Representative in Congress should vote if none of the candidates received an Electoral College majority. The respondents split their choices among the options they were offered. Their Representative should vote for the candidate:

With the most popular votes nationwide	29%
Who carries your state	16%
Who carries your congressional district	14%
Who would make the best president	33%
Don't know, no answer	7%

Gallup national telephone survey of 1,006 adults, August 1995.

22. Longley and Braun, 154.

23. Shlomo Slonin, "The Electoral College at Philadelphia: The Evolution of an Ad Hoc Congress for the Selection of a President," *Journal of American History* 73 (June 1986): 35–58, cited in Ellis, 110.

24. Longley and Braun, 169.

CHAPTER 5. *How Well Does the Constitutional System Perform?*

1. I have drawn feely here from my "Thinking About Democratic Constitutions: Conclusions from Democratic Experience," in Ian Shapiro and Russell Hardin, eds., *NOMOS XXXVIII, Political Order* (New York: New York University Press, 1996).

2. The survival of basic democratic institutions should not be confused with the stability or turnover of parliamentary "governments." Parliamentary systems display a huge variation in the durability of cabinet coalitions—"governments"—ranging among our twenty two democratic countries from the relatively high turnover of cabinets in Italy to their much higher stability in Norway and Britain. Even in Italy, however, an outgoing cabinet may return with essentially the same members and parties represented in the government.

3. Mathew Soberg Shugart and John M. Carey, *Presidents and Assemblies: Constitutional Design and Electoral Dynamics* (Cambridge: Cambridge University Press, 1992), 41.

4. Support for this view and also more skeptical views may be found in Juan Linz and Arturo Valenzuela, eds., *The Failure of Presidential Democracy: Comparative Perspectives*, vol. 1 (Baltimore: Johns Hopkins University Press, 1994).

5. Shugart and Carey, 42.

6. Aili Piano and Arch Puddington, "The 2000 Freedom House Survey," *Journal of Democracy* 12 (January 2001): 87–92.

7. Freedom House, *Press Freedom Survey: Press Freedom World Wide* (January 1, 1999).

8. Here I follow the usage in G. Bingham Powell, Jr., *Elections as Instruments of Democracy* (New Haven: Yale University Press, 2000).

9. An excellent analysis supported by extensive analysis and data is provided by Powell, *Elections*.

10. See ibid., Chs. 4 and 6.

11. Ibid., 129, 130, 197.

12. Arend Lijphart, Democracies, *Patterns of Majoritarian and Consensus Government in Twenty-One Countries* (New Haven: Yale University Press, 1984), and *Patterns of Democracy, Government Forms and Performance in Thirty-Six Countries* (New Haven: Yale University Press, 1999).

13. Hans Daalder, "The Netherlands: Opposition in a Segmented Society," in Robert A. Dahl, ed., *Political Oppositions in Western Democracies* (New Haven: Yale University Press, 1966), 188–236; Arend Lijphart, *The Politics of Accommoda-*

tion: Pluralism and Democracy in the Netherlands, 2nd rev. ed. (Berkeley: University of California Press, 1975), 104ff.

14. Leif Leiwin, "Majoritarian and Consensus Democracy: The Swedish Experience," *Scandinavian Political Studies* 21, no. 3 (1988): 195–206.

15. Christopher J. Anderson and Christine A. Guillory, "Political Institutions and Satisfaction with Democracy: A Cross-National Analysis of Consensus and Majoritarian Systems," *American Political Science Review* 91, (March 199): 66–81.

16. Ibid., fig. 4, p. 77.

17. Ibid., 78.

18. David R. Mayhew, *Divided We Govern: Party Control, Lawmaking, and Investigations, 1946–1990* (New Haven: Yale University Press, 1991), 1.

19. Ibid., 76.

20. John J. Coleman, "Unified Government, Divided Government, and Party Responsiveness," *American Political Science Review* 93 (December 1999): 821–36.

21. Jeffrey K. Tulis, *The Rhetorical Presidency* (Princeton: Princeton University Press, 1987), 87ff. Gil Troy, "Candidates Take the Stump, Then and Now," letter, *New York Times,* January 17, 1988.

22. I have examined these at greater length in "The Myth of the Presidential Mandate," *Political Science Quarterly* 105 (Fall 1990): 355–72.

23. Fred I. Greenstein, "The Benevolent Leader: Children's Images of Political Authority," *American Political Science Review* 54 (December 1960): 934–43. The views of American school children about the president differ from those of British and French school children about their chief executives. "Children and Politics in Britain, France, and the United States: Six Examples," Fred I. Greenstein and Sidney Tarrow, *Youth and Society* 2 (1970): 111–28.

24. Edward Tufte and I undertook such an inquiry in *Size and Democracy* (Stanford: Stanford University Press, 1975) but regrettably the topic seems not to have attracted much subsequent investigation.

25. Dahl and Tufte, *Size and Democracy,* 95ff.

26. Though on a Purchasing Power Parity Basis, the difference diminishes to less than four times. U.S. Census Bureau, *Statistical Abstract of the United States, The National Data Book, 1999* (Washington, D.C.: U.S. Government Printing Office, 1999), 841, Table 1362.

27. For more details, see Table 5.1, Appendix.

28. Lijphart (1999), supra, 301-2.

29. Juan Linz and Alfred Stepan provide impressive evidence that by providing more points at which privileged minorities can veto the enactment of federal polices, the American federal system is the worst performer on social policies among all of the OECD countries. A brief preliminary version of their findings is "Inequality Inducing and Inequality Reducing Federalism: With Special Reference to the 'Classic Outlier'—the USA," paper prepared for the XVIII World Congress of the International Political Science Association, August 1-5, 2000, Quebec City, Canada.

CHAPTER 6. *Why Not a More Democratic Constitution?*

1. Michael Schudson, *The Good Citizen, A History of American Civic Life* (Cambridge, Mass.: Harvard University Press, 1998), 202.

2. Constitutional Knowledge Survey, National Constitutional Center, September, 1997, question 2.

3. Gallup Organization, 1999.

4. In the following sections I have drawn freely on my essay "The Future of Political Equality," in Keith Dowding, James Hughes, and Helen Margetts, eds., *Challenges to Democracy* (Hampshire, U.K.: Palgrave, 2001).

5. For a full account of failures to provide equal citizenship among Americans, see Rogers M. Smith's masterly work, *Civic Ideals: Conflicting Visions of Citizenship in U S. History* (New Haven: Yale University Press, 1997).

6. Probably because he was heavily in debt, he freed only five slaves on his death. Annette Gordon-Reed, *Thomas Jefferson and Sally Hemings: An American Controversy* (Charlottesville: University of Virginia Press, 1997), 38. Although his reasons for freeing these five are unclear, all were related to his

mistress, Sally Hemings, and two were probably sons by her. Although the issue of paternity is disputed, Gordon-Reed provides strong circumstantial evidence. For her "Summary of the Evidence," see 210ff and see also Appendix B, "The Memoirs of Madison Hemings," 245ff. DNA tests provide additional circumstantial, though not conclusive, evidence. See Dinitia Smith and Nicholas Wade, "DNA Test Finds Evidence of Jefferson Child by Slave," *New York Times*, November 1, 1998.

7. New York: Schocken Books, 1961, Henry Reeve, trans., vol. 1, p. lxxxi.

8. I have drawn these estimates from Adrian Karatnycky, "The 1999 Freedom House Survey: A Century of Progress," *Journal of Democracy* 11, no. 1 (January 2000): 187–200; Robert A. Dahl, *Democracy and Its Critics* (New Haven: Yale University Press, 1989): Table 17.2, p. 240; and Tatu Vanhanen, *The Emergence of Democracy: A Comparative Study of 119 States, 1850–1879* (Helsinki: Finnish Academy of Sciences and Letters, 1984), Table 22, p. 120.

9. As one example, he writes, that "among the untouchables of India there is persuasive evidence that the Hindu doctrines that would legitimize caste domination are negated, reinterpreted, or ignored. Scheduled castes are much less likely than Brahmins to believe that the doctrine of karma explains their present condition; instead they attribute their status to their poverty and to an original, mythical act of injustice." *Domination and the Arts of Resistance* (New Haven: Yale University Press, 1990), 117.

10. The late Joseph Hamburger showed that to secure the expansion of the suffrage (and ultimately the passage of the Reform Act of 1832), James Mill, though opposed to violence as a means, deliberately set out to create a fear of revolution among members of the oligarchy. "Since Mill wished to achieve fundamental reforms without violence, it became necessary to devise means by which an oligarchy would be led to grant concessions out of self-interest. . . . [T]here were only two alternatives: '[The people] can only obtain any considerable amelioration in their government by resistance, by applying physical force to their rulers, or at least, by threats so likely

to be followed by performance, as may frighten their rulers into compliance.' Since the use of physical force was to be avoided, Mill built his hopes on the second alternative. . . . Mill was proposing that revolution be threatened. He assumed that the threat would be sufficient and that it would not be necessary to carry it out." *James Mill and the Art of Revolution* (New Haven: Yale University Press, 1963), 23–24.

11. I provide a fuller account in *Democracy and Its Critics*, 84ff. There and elsewhere I have drawn on Stanley I. Benn, "Egalitarianism and the Equal Consideration of Interests," in J. R. Pennock and J. W. Chapman, *Equality (Nomos IX)* (New York: Atherton, 1967), 61–78.

12. This assumption is more fully developed in *Democracy and Its Critics*, 105ff, and restated in briefer form in *On Democracy* (New Haven: Yale University Press, 1998), 74ff.

13. For an excellent analysis, see Amartya Sen, *Inequality Rexamined* (Cambridge, Mass.: Harvard University Press, 1992). "Libertarians," he writes, "must think it important that people should have liberty. Given this, questions would immediately arise regarding *who, how much, how distributed, how equal.* Thus the issue of equality immediately arises as a supplement to the assertion of the importance of liberty." (22)

14. These sentences are a close paraphrase of his statements in 1: 298, 304, and 2: 380–81.

CHAPTER 7. *Some Reflections on the Prospects for a More Democratic Constitution*

1. CBS News/*New York Times* telephone poll of 1,254 adults, May 1987, question 53.

2. See also Amartya Sen, *Inequality Reexamined*, 36–37 and *passim*. Ronald Dworkin, "What Is Equality? Part 2: Equality of Resources," *Philosophy and Public Affairs* 10 (1981).

3. *Buckley v. Valeo*, 424 U.S. 1 (1976).

4. For an extended argument consistent with my brief comments, see John Hart Ely, *Democracy and Distrust: A Theory of Judicial Review* (Cambridge, Mass.: Harvard University Press, 1980).

CHAPTER 8. *Further Reflections*

1. In what is probably the most famous book on the subject, Walter Bagehot confidently described the main features of "the English Constitution" without ever mentioning that these were nowhere prescribed in a single, written, constitutional document. Cf. *The English Constitution* (1867).

2. Documents cited thus are listed in full at the end of this chapter, under "For Further Reading."

3. Evidence for the three propositions will be found in chapters 3–7, 44–222.

4. In the last free elections, in July, 1932, the Nazi party, the NSDAP, received only 37 percent of the vote and in November 1932 even less, 33 percent (Dolf Sternberger and Bernhard Vogel, *Die Wahl Der Parlamenta* [Berlin: Walter De Gruyter, 1969], vol. 1, table A 11:358).

5. "Most legislative races lacked any meaningful competition. Only four U.S. House incumbents lost to non-incumbent challengers in their severely gerrymandered districts, the average House race was won by a victory margin of more than 40% and more than four out of every five U.S. House races were won by landslide margins of 20% or more and more than nine out of every ten races were won by a margin of more than 10%. In state legislative elections from 1998–2002, two of every five winners faced no major party opposition, including 37% of this year's winners." (www.fairvote.org/e-news/20021114.htm)

6. More details will be found in Reynolds and Reilly, 1997; Hill, 2002; Thompson, 2002; and Amy, 2002. See also www.fairvote.org.

7. Constitutional scholars have also shown how the undemocratic consequences of winner take all in the electoral college could be corrected without a constitutional amendment if the legislatures of the eleven largest states, which now have a majority of votes in the electoral college, were all to enact legislation requiring their delegates to the electoral college to cast their votes for the candidate with a majority of the popular votes. (Amar and Amar, 2001; Bennett, 2002). Combining this with preferential voting, or instant runoff, would ensure that a majority of popular votes would be required to elect the president. (Amar and Amar, 2002)

Appendix A

1. *The Federalist* (New York: Modern Library, n.d.), 59.

2. Willi Paul Adams, *The First American Constitutions: Republican Ideology and the Making of State Constitutions in the Revolutionary Era* (Chapel Hill: University of North Carolina Press, 1980), 106ff.

3. "The Federalist No. 39," in *The Federalist, op. cit.*, 242ff.

4. Montesquieu, *De l'Esprit des Lois*, Tome I (Paris: Editions Garnier Fräres, 1961), Bk 2, Ch. 2, p. 12.

5. Ibid., Bk. 8, Ch. 16, p. 131. One might expect the reason for this conclusion to lie in the difficulty of assembling the people in a large territory. But in direct contradiction to Madison's later argument in Federalist No.10 that the danger of factionalism would be reduced by increasing the size of the political unit, Montesquieu contended that in a large republic the common good would suffer. "In a little (republic), the common good is better felt, better known, and closer to each citizen."

6. Bernard Bailyn, ed., *Debate on the Constitution*, 2 vols. (New York: Library of America, 1992), 1:803–04.

7. James F. Simon, *What Kind of Nation? Thomas Jefferson, John Marshall, and the Epic Struggle to Create a United States* (New York: Simon and Schuster, 2002), 25.

8. For further discussion, see my *Pluralist Democracy in the United States* (Chicago: Rand McNally, 1967), 34ff.

For Further Reading

Amar, Akhil Reed, and Amar, Vikram David. "The 2000 Election and the Electoral College." *FindLaw's Legal Commentary*, part 1, Nov. 30, 2001; part 2, Dec. 14, 2001; part 3, Dec. 28, 2001.

———. "The Fatal Flaw in France's—and America's—Voting System, and How an 'Instant Runoff' System Might Remedy It." *FindLaw's Legal Commentary*, May 3, 2002.

Amy, Douglas J. *Real Choices/New Voices: How Proportional Representation Elections Could Revitalize American Democracy.* 2d ed. New York: Columbia University Press, 2002.

Bennett, Robert W. "Popular Election of the President Without a Constitutional Amendment." *The Green Bag*, no. 3 (Spring 2001): 241–46.

———. "State Coordination in Popular Election of the President Without a Constitutional Amendment." *The Green Bag*, no. 2 (Winter 2002), 141–49.

Dahl, Robert A. "Decision-Making in a Democracy: The Supreme Court as a National Policy-Maker." *Journal of Public*

Law 6, no. 2 (1958), 279–95. Reprinted in *Emory Law Journal* 50 (Spring 2000), 563–82.

Hill, Steven. *Fixing Elections: The Failure of America's Winner Take All Politics.* New York: Routledge, 2002.

Lazare, Daniel. *The Frozen Republic: How the Constitution Is Paralyzing Democracy.* New York: Harcourt Brace, 1996.

Lee, Frances I., and Bruce I. Oppenheimer. *Sizing Up the Senate: The Unequal Consequences of Equal Representation.* Chicago: University of Chicago Press, 1999.

Reynolds, Andrew, and Ben Reilly. *The International IDEA Handbook of Electoral System Design.* Stockholm: International Institute for Democracy and Electoral Assistance, 1997.

Rosenberg, Gerald N. *The Hollow Hope: Can Courts Bring About Social Change?* Chicago: University of Chicago Press, 1991.

Sandler, Ross, and David Schoenbrod. *Democracy by Decree: What Happens When Courts Run Government?* New Haven: Yale University Press: 2002.

Shugart, Mathew Soberg, and Martin P. Wattenberg. *Mixed Member Electoral Systems: The Best of Both Worlds?* Oxford: Oxford University Press, 2001.

Thompson, Dennis F. *Just Elections: Creating a Fair Electoral Process in the United States.* Chicago: University of Chicago Press, 2002.

Website:
www.fairvote.org

Index